Sins of the
Father

SHANEDA DALY

WITH LINDA WATSON-BROWN

Sins of the Father

ABUSED BY MY FATHER EVERY DAY FOR A DECADE, THIS IS MY STORY OF SURVIVAL

JB

First published in the UK by John Blake Publishing
An imprint of Bonnier Books UK
4th Floor, Victoria House
Bloomsbury Square
London WC1B 4DA
England

Owned by Bonnier Books
Sveavägen 56, Stockholm, Sweden

www.facebook.com/johnblakebooks
twitter.com/jblakebooks

Trade Paperback ISBN: 978-1-789-464-66-5
Ebook ISBN: 978-1-789-464-67-2
Audiobook ISBN: 978-1-789-464-68-9

A CIP catalogue of this book is available from the British Library.

Design by www.envydesign.co.uk

Printed and bound in Great Britain by Clays Ltd, Elcograf S.p.A.

1 3 5 7 9 10 8 6 4 2

This book is a work of non-fiction, based on the life, experiences and recollections of Shaneda Daly. Certain details in this story, including names and locations, have been changed to protect the identity and privacy of the author, their family and those mentioned.

John Blake Publishing is an imprint of Bonnier Books UK
www.bonnierbooks.co.uk

For Imelda

*You always loved me, you were always there for me,
my Mommy Melda, my rock x*

And for everyone who reads this book, remember this:

*Just because you've been pushed into the fire doesn't
mean you'll burn. Take strength from those flames and
forge your own path. You are a warrior.*

Contents

Prologue

I'm not sure I could even describe what it had been like inside the court – the details had all been such a blur, washing over me as I sat there. I had spent most of it avoiding looking at him, pulling my hair over my face so that he couldn't see me – so that the judge couldn't see me either. The things that were read out, the things that were spoken, turned my stomach. It had all been done to me, but the thought that everything was being laid out for everyone else to hear was almost too much.

I knew I was right and I knew this was the place where I would finally see him face justice and yet it was terrifying. My legs were like jelly, shaking uncontrollably. My hands couldn't stop trembling, I was shivering. I'd hidden behind my partner for most of the trial but now I took a deep breath and slowly peeked through my curtain of hair.

He stood there with his head held high. The big I am.

Harry Daly.

My father.

My abuser.

I heard words that I knew the meaning of but not the impact, as if I was falling into a fog, grasping onto some things but not being able to make sense of what was happening.

Guilty.

Ten years.

Fifteen years.

Concurrent sentences.

And then there was a slip of time. I was coming out of the court into the spiral of the main hall, that round bright space which holds the fate of so many inside its walls. I grounded myself to the moment by counting the people around me as I wondered what was going on. Fifteen. There were fifteen.

And then it hit me.

My God, I'm still alive. I've come this far and lived. I've done this. Me. Only me.

I'd survived.

I can't change where I came from, but I can decide where I'm going.

This is my story of how I got there.

CHAPTER 1

Beginnings

I've always said that you can't tell where you're going unless you know where you've been – and that goes back to before any of us were born. We all face choices in life where we look at two paths coming off the same road and while I've always tried to take the right one, there's no doubt that there were those who attempted to push me down others.

Writing my story has made me think back to everything that went before me, the foundations that were laid, the people and places I came from. In Ireland, you'll never go short of someone telling you a tale and here's mine.

My maternal grandparents lived in a little place called Coill Dubh in County Kildare, about twenty-five miles from Dublin. The village was specially built for the men who were going to be working on the bog nearby, cutting peat to supply the local power station. There were about a hundred homes there, a little community of its own.

The women in particular were in and out of every house all the time and they had a real bond. They even helped each other deliver their babies as no one went to hospital in those days. It was a very hard way of life and one which the women held together. They cooked, they cleaned, they raised the children and made sure everything hung together.

When I remember my Nanny Rooney who lived in one of those little houses, she was always working, apron on, covered in flour, washing the floors or making soup. Always busy, never taking a rest or even a bit of time for herself.

And they never stopped having babies.

Mom was the middle child of thirteen, six siblings either side of her. It was a poor family, they struggled, but they seem to have had a happy childhood. I'm very close to one of Mom's younger sisters, my Aunt Imelda, and she's told me that there was nothing sinister or cruel about their upbringing, it was all quite straightforward.

Mom – Rose – was born in 1956. With my grandmother at home all the time there was always someone there, she wasn't some sort of latchkey kid. I know that Nanny looked after them all well, she made all their clothes herself and made sure they were well fed. There were no luxuries but they had as good a life as they could with the little they had.

There were so many of them that they were all at

different stages of their lives. Mom's youngest sister is only nine years younger than me and the eldest is in their seventies. The older crowd was leaving as the younger ones were being born. Nanny was obsessed with her boys and thought that they could do no wrong – anything they did was just boys being boys, according to her. She'd have let them away with anything and often did.

Although they didn't have much, they were kind people. One of my cousins remembers Nanny Rooney and Grandad Dan often turning up at their house with bags of food, as well as sacks of turf for heating, never coming empty-handed. Nanny was very close to her sisters and they always had a good bond. The message was that family mattered – I was to discover it only mattered under certain conditions.

When I was small, I would travel from Dublin with my family to see them all and Nanny was always waiting at the door for me – she was a big, chubby woman, a real traditional granny, and when she wrapped me in her arms, I could feel her folds of fat! It was lovely, warm and comforting, and just what you'd want when you're little. Nanny Rooney ended up with sixty grandchildren and she made each of us feel as important as the next one, just as loved, just as special.

My Grandad Dan is the only man in my life I have ever met who I would call a perfect gentleman. Always quiet and thoughtful, he'd sit there and just nod along to everything.

Nanny was the boss but they were both wonderful. They were such a source of love for me and I believe that they had been the same way with Mom as she grew up. Even when we moved and lived 140 miles away from them, they wrote to each other all the time. There was a real strong sense of family there, a good solid background – different to my dad's in a lot of ways.

My dad Harry was from Dublin with a father who was in the Army, just as he would end up. Other people tell me that my grandfather was really stern but he died when I was six, so I don't have too many of my own recollections of him. The main thing I remember was that he always bought me ice cream – and when you're little, that's about one of the best memories you can have! He liked me and my little brother, Alan, most out of all of his grandchildren and he was completely open about that.

'Do you love us the most, Grandad?' I would ask him.

'Sure, why wouldn't I?' he'd reply. 'You're the only ones who have my name, not like your cousins!'

My other grandmother was the complete opposite of Nanny Rooney. Lilly Daly had plastic covering over everything so that it wouldn't get messed up. From the moment I stepped in her front door, I was terrified in case I ruined something.

'Take your shoes off!' she'd say as soon as she opened the door. 'Watch where you're going!'

I'd tiptoe along the corridor, which had a thick, dimpled

covering over the pristine carpet, into the living room, where all the furniture was covered in more plastic.

'Are you clean?' she'd ask, squinting at me. It wouldn't have mattered if I was covered in mud, given that I wasn't allowed to touch anything. 'Sit on that chair – and don't do ANYTHING.' That kitchen table was where I would spend the whole visit, not even allowed to speak; not that I would have, she was so intimidating.

There was one year when my brother Alan and I had given up sugar for Lent because Dad had, but when we went to Granny's, she put sugar in our tea. We wouldn't have dared tell her, so we drank the tea. She was higher up than God in our eyes and she'd be worse to cross, so Lent had to take a back seat in her kitchen.

Lilly was a cold, thin woman who never hugged me, never made me feel welcome. There was only ever the slightest sliver of affection on one occasion much later in my life. One of Dad's brothers-in-law, Joe, died when I was in my early twenties and when she saw me at the funeral, she put her hand up to my face and said, 'Oh Shanny, you look gorgeous.'

I remember saying to someone, 'Jesus Christ, that's the first time she's ever touched me and it felt more like a slap, but I suppose she was trying!'

After my Grandad Henry died in 1980 and we visited, she'd always try and get rid of me so that she could have Dad to herself. I'd be sent to the corner shop to get her cigarettes – I was six or seven at the time, but that was perfectly normal back then – and I knew that I should take my time as they wouldn't want me sitting with them, getting in the way.

'Are you back already?' I'd be asked, even if I'd been gone for hours. 'Sit there, don't move.'

These different families produced very different people in my parents. Dad was confident, sure of himself, always thinking he was superior to everyone else. It was the opposite for Mom. All the women in her family were so opinionated and strong, but not her. She was and still is a little mouse compared to 'The Women' as all the others are known as one group amongst our lot. Her three older sisters would carry themselves into a room with pride. You would always know they were there. They'd waltz in, heads up, straight at you with their opinions, which Mom would never do for fear of someone disagreeing with her. In a big family like that, everyone would be ripping into everyone else and they'd change their opinion from one day to the next so there was no point in trying to guess which way the wind blew – and that resulted in Mom just keeping quiet. Maybe she thought she was being a good little girl, but it would have actually been the opposite sort of character that was seen as completely normal in that environment.

Margaret, the eighth oldest, was the wildest of them all. She left home for Dublin and never went back, married and pregnant and setting out her own life. My grandparents never even attended her wedding so she must have been even more difficult than the others. Margaret and Imelda were younger than Mom and they both knew what feisty meant.

One of my aunts once said to me, 'Your mother was always a whingey bitch,' but that was just the way they spoke about each other.

I think, in a huge family like theirs, you could always have missed out on a few things that you should have been noticing. If you've that many kids, there's no way you can look after them emotionally. Someone's going to get lost at some time and maybe that's what happened to Mom. If you have two kids getting married at one end of the scale and two others making Communion at the other, there's only so much attention you can give to it all.

All the girls in her family got sent away to Dublin to work when they turned eighteen. A few of them worked in hospitals, a few in cleaning, and they would send home a few bob from their wages. Mom always sent money back but when she asked her younger sister Margaret if she was going to do that when she got to Dublin, she got a very different point of view: 'Oh, they can fuck off if they're expecting that!' Margaret told her. 'I'll be keeping my own money for myself.'

The only job Mom ever told me about was when she had worked in a shop and the owners hadn't allowed her to go home after her sister Imelda's baby had been lost to cot death. She never spoke of any other work she did, but Dad certainly told me another story, of a time when she worked in a pub.

He was at a dance hall in Dublin one night when a fire broke out. The whole place was evacuated and he went into the nearest bar to get away from it all. And there was Mom. It's funny when you hear about how your parents got together, how their story started without you in it, especially when you know where that story is going. That night, from a fire in a dance hall, from an unplanned walk into a bar, came everything I've ever known.

I can picture it now.

Dad would walk in with his Dublin swagger, looking like he owned the place, and he would have spotted Mom working at the bar.

'How are ye?' he would have said and that would have been the start. It all came from there. He would have been full of bravado and she fell for it.

I was eight when I realised Mom must have been pregnant when they got married. I did the arithmetic and boldly said to her, 'You were already having me when you got married, isn't that right, Mammy?'

'Well, you can count – what do you expect me to say?'

'Were you having me as a baby, Mom?' I asked again.

'Yes, yes, I was.'

It was no secret, there was no shame – she didn't go into any detail though, I wasn't spun a story about how I was the icing on the cake for their love. However, I wasn't told to keep it quiet and I don't think they had hidden it back then either. She must have got pregnant straight away as the wedding had been about six months after they first met, with Mom already three or four months gone. It was love at first sight; to this day, they're like something out of Mills & Boon, holding hands, wrapped up in each other, and I can't imagine it would have been any different back then.

She was only eighteen when they met and Dad was twenty-one. He'd already lived a bit whereas she knew County Kildare and not much else. The very fact that he was from Dublin would have brought a complete imbalance to their relationship. Dublin is the capital of Ireland and by God, do Dubliners make the most of that. They have egos the size of the moon! When I was young, I would actually vomit if I had to go to a family event with my Dubliner cousins. They were so much classier and knew everything, they were more beautiful with lovely clothes and it just made me feel sick to the stomach that they would be judging me. It was all in my head that they would. Everyone was actually always so nice to me when I did see them, however I'd always feel inferior to everyone else. I think I kind of felt removed from the family circle when we lived far away and I overthought what they would think of me when we did meet up – would I seem stupid or would I not fit in? Would they feel I wasn't part of the 'real' family and that I behaved in some sort of way that they looked down on?

Going back, I'd think Mom would be a bit in awe of this Dublin lad too. He was always a charismatic bullshitter was Harry Daly, nothing's changed. On top of the Dublin shine, he was the golden boy in my granny's eyes. They were middle-class with my Grandad's Army background and a house they had bought, rather than rented. It was just a three-bedroomed terrace, but absolutely pristine with really nice things. They were the first on the road to have a TV and it was thought of as a cut above that they had their own car too.

Dad didn't go without anything and was indulged for all of his life.

'Would you like me to sort your egg for you there now, Harry?' Lilly Daly would ask when we visited. A grown man, getting his mother to take the top off his boiled egg!

Even when he was married, he wouldn't allow his dinner to be reheated as he'd always had his mother dancing attendance on him, making sure everything was a perfect temperature just when he wanted it.

'Now, Rose,' he would say to his wife, 'that's not how it's done. It's not what I'm used to.' That would progress throughout the years when he would often just refuse to eat what Mom put in front of him, pushing it away and heading off for a takeaway. She accepted it like she accepted everything he did. If it was Harry doing it, she would still adore him, no matter how he was behaving – and, by God, would she eventually take that to extremes.

Lilly closed her eyes to a lot of things where he was involved, but I think Grandad Henry had the measure of him. When Dad was fourteen, his father forged his birth certificate to get him into the English Navy. I've seen the photograph of him in his uniform and, honest to God, he looks about eleven, so there must have been a lot of denial and desperation around that. A cousin told me that the reason Henry was so keen to get rid of him was that Dad had sexually abused a younger family member and he wanted him sent away. His whole family is shut down so for me to even be told that about him is a huge thing.

This was the man my mother fell in love with, this big lump of superiority who was to be the love of her life. She'd never been with anyone else and for her, this was it. The scene was set – it was just waiting for the curtain to be completely lifted on The Harry Show.

CHAPTER TWO

Love

They moved in together before they got married, with Mom not getting her dream of a fairy-tale wedding given that she was pregnant. She had never wanted it to be under those circumstances, and said 'no' to him a few times, but she also wouldn't have wanted to be an unmarried mother. It was an odd thing because there had never been any shame in our family about that and I discovered why when I was a bit older.

When I was sixteen, I found out that Nanny Rooney had been in a Mother and Baby Home. These were institutions where unmarried, pregnant women and young girls were sent, usually just for the 'sin' of having a baby outside of wedlock. As the years have passed, more and more horrific stories have emerged of the cruelties that went on in these places. In 2015, it was actually uncovered that hundreds of babies had been buried in unmarked graves in County Galway. Before she'd had any of the thirteen that I knew about, Nanny had another baby in one of those homes. She was one of the lucky ones: she got out with her baby, who was then brought up as Mom's aunt, reared by her own grandparents. It's a terrible dark time in Ireland's history and the story could have been very different.

Nanny's experiences were why she never gave out to any of them about babies or sex.

She always said to anyone who told her that their daughter or granddaughter was pregnant but not married, 'Sure, they could be coming in, telling you they have cancer or AIDS, and you'd be losing them. A baby is nothing.' This was before I even knew her story – it was just something she was firm on, no matter what.

I once asked her, 'How did you get away with not having to get married with that baby?'

'My mother would rather send me away than have anyone know I was pregnant and not married, that's the truth,' she told me.

The whole control of the Irish Catholic Church was more powerful than anything else, more powerful than looking after your own daughter and her baby, more important than keeping them at your side. With all we now know about those homes, the thought of Nanny being sent to one makes my blood run cold.

Grandad Dan got to know the father of her child in later years and that man told him that he had always wanted to marry her but the families wouldn't allow it. It was easier to send her away. However, they hadn't accounted for the sort of woman she was and once in the home, she refused to sign a single document. They kept pressing her to sign her baby away for adoption, all through the pregnancy and afterwards, but she just wouldn't do it.

The moment she had her child, Nanny was told by the nuns to get out of bed and get her work done, that there was to be no lazing about for someone like her.

'I remember my head spinning as I sat up,' she told me. 'As my feet hit the cold tiled floor, the blood poured from me and I haemorrhaged. Jesus, I thought my insides were after falling out! They took the baby away from me and pushed some papers in my face. If I'd signed those, that would have been it. She'd have been given away, I'd have no say in it.'

Nanny stayed there for a year and a half, barely seeing her daughter Moira, working her fingers to the bone until she managed to leave. I was told that my great-grandad Whelan, Nanny's father, sent his son to get them both out of the home when the little one was about eighteen months. It was as if he'd just remembered they were there. I have no idea why he did that then, why he didn't think to do it when the baby was younger – maybe it was a punishment that he kept going for a while. I don't have much more about the story than that, but I always wondered if that was what made Nanny so strong. She was some character, a woman who would as soon tell you to fuck off as give you a hug, and I feel that she runs through every part of who I am.

I don't really know much about Mom's pregnancy, it was never the sort of thing where she sat me on her knee and told me warm stories about how she loved me before I was even born. All I know is that she went into the hospital when she was overdue and the doctor said that she'd have to be induced. She agreed to it all but had no idea what that meant.

'What's he on about?' she asked her mother, straight to the phone box as soon as she had left the consulting room. Nanny Rooney would probably have told her to shut up and get on with it. The only other thing Mom told me was that the obstetrician had arthritis in his hand and when he did an internal examination, it was agony as he was all over the place and couldn't feel what his own hands were doing. That stayed with me a long time whenever I thought about having babies.

The place we were living in when I was born was an awful tip, there were even rats scratching about behind the walls.

'What are you doing, Harry?' Mom would ask when Dad sat up at night.

'Christ, have you not heard them today, Rose? The

bastards think they own the place! I'm watching out in case they break through the fecking wall and bite Shanny in her cot.'

It was a normal family life back then and they just wanted to carry on with things in a better house. They were on lists to try and get a different council or corporation rental and waited each day as it was the milkman or postman who would come with such news. It wasn't until my brother Alan was born, a year after me, that a three-bedroom property came up in Ballymun. It was almost unheard of for anyone to get a place like that, there was rarely any availability, which meant that when my parents heard it was theirs, they wanted to get to it immediately. The story goes that they piled everything into the pram – pots, plates, everything they had – and ran off to get the keys before going straight there. No time for a van, just get there, away from the rats, as soon as they could.

A few years after we left, Ballymun turned into junkie city, but at the time it seemed fine. We lived on the seventh floor of an eight-storey flat, with one auntie five minutes across the road and another just by the shopping centre nearby. There was a family feeling to life when I was little and a lot of laughter when everyone got together, even if Mom did sit like a mouse, not really joining in with things.

Growing up, we always had the best of toys, which was no surprise as that was my parents' attitude to everything. Harry Daly had to have the best of the best and Rose just went along with whatever the man of her dreams wanted. There might be no food in the cupboard but people would see that, on the outside, we had all the things that money could buy. It was a weird obsession and it lasted all the time I was at home. We had a CD player years before anyone else, it was a badge of honour for them to have any mod con first amongst the people who knew them. Satellite dishes, the best clothes for Alan and me, but at the same time, the electricity would be cut off and there wasn't so much as a crust of bread in the press. There are photos of us all dressed up in the fanciest clothes, holding expensive toys, and that was all that mattered to our parents, to Harry really – that we looked the part. It was an image of something that wasn't real. We had everything material even if we had nothing in our bellies and that has to be a sign of something rotten at the heart of a family. Even when there was food, I was never allowed in the kitchen or fridge without permission and no matter how hungry I was, I would have to wait until something was given to me.

'I'm starving, Mom,' I would often say.

Her usual reply was, 'So?'

Each day, Dad would go off to work in his green uniform, looking very smart and presenting a respectable front to all of the community. The reliable soldier, the Army man. One day, he came back with a red sports bag with stripes on it that I now know was Adidas – the labels always mattered. The leather bag was moving from the inside, which made Alan and me completely confused. Dad unzipped it and brought out two German Shepherd puppies. The other soldiers had been kicking them about and they had come home to us. Mom made them a little corner in one of the bedrooms with teddies all around the edges and an alarm clock in there so that the ticking would make them think it was their mother's heartbeat. She fed them with a bottle and really did take good care of them. One was black and the other was brown, and with a complete lack of imagination, we called them Blackie and Brownie – probably like a hundred other dogs on the estate. Mom was affectionate with those puppies, more than she ever was with me and Alan, and it was another sign of us being a proper family to anyone on the outside looking in.

I remember Mom had this mad green coat with a big fur collar all the way round, it made her look like Elsie Tanner from *Coronation Street*. She would wear a bit of make-up, which was all too tempting for me and Alan to mess about with if we got the chance, and had brown shoulder-length hair that she would get set at the hairdresser, making it all springy and fake. Actually, she was a few *Coronation Street* characters because she'd turn into Gail Platt when she was in a bad mood, all funny chin and bouncy hair.

Rose did have friends, but she was still the mousey one when we did go visiting. She was still young, only in her twenties, but compared to all my aunties, compared even to my grandmother, she was like an old woman. Obsessed with Harry, only waiting on the times when they could sit on the sofa together, cuddled up, kissing and smooching, seemingly oblivious to me and my little brother. Jesus, the pair of them made me feel so nauseous, or, as I would have said, gave me the boak (our way of saying nauseous).

There was definitely a face they put on for other people though. While Dad was the respectable, good-natured one, and Mom was the ideal wife with the spotless house, the way they treated me and Alan was far from perfect, even at that stage. There is no point in my life that I can't remember us both being locked in rooms for hours on end, full days sometimes and usually with nothing in our bellies. If you can't remember when something started, then you know it must have been at an awful young age.

I do know that I had a Fisher-Price toy I loved that I used to have in there with me and I wouldn't have had something like that unless I had been very small. If it was Alan's room which held us, we'd upturn his bed onto the side so that just the springs showed and we would pretend it was the zoo. Thank God we had imaginations. I have more memories of being locked in rooms together with him than being outside of those rooms. I don't think it was even for punishment a lot of the time, it was just how they dealt with it. Were we annoying? Did we interfere with their Mills & Boon romance? Who knows?

The words I heard most from Mom's mouth were,

'Wait till your father gets home.' He'd hardly be in the door before she'd be telling him how much of a pain we had been – even when we hadn't.

'Oh Harry, what a day I've had – they've been terrible, the pair of them. You'll have to do something about it.'

And he did. He always did.

I got hit a lot for wetting the bed. He'd pull my pants down, slap me or go at me with his belt and all that did was to make me wet the bed again that night through fear. He was very fond of a bamboo stick that he kept and I can feel that on my arse to this day. But he'd use anything that came to hand, he wasn't choosy.

The irony was, most of those days were ones that Mom spent in bed as soon as Dad left the house. I'm not denying we got up to some things – we set fire to a teddy one day with candles we found, we flooded the flat many a time – but we wouldn't have done any of that if she'd been watching us or playing with us rather than lying in her bed all day.

We were in that flat in Ballymun for three years and Rose spent a hell of a lot of that time in her bed. I honestly don't know whether she was ill, depressed or just plain lazy. She certainly had enough energy to get up as soon as Dad came back and make sure that he whipped the arses off us for something we probably hadn't even done that day. I don't know what I would have felt if Alan hadn't been there. My happy memories are of playing with him or with my cousins. I loved family get-togethers at Christmas (they'd become the only good memories I had of that time of year) and I wanted that feeling all the time. We'd sometimes go over to Coolock in the Northside of Dublin, where Dad's older sister, Debra, lived. That was a wonderland because her husband worked for Cadbury's and there was a whole press full of chocolate and I'd be sent home with bags of it.

Happiness was there at times, I won't deny it, but Mom would put a stop to it when she could. One time, Dad was in the bath and he called both of us to the room. Alan and I were still dressed, but he dragged the two of us in with him. There was lots of roaring and laughing going on before Mom got there, shouting.

'What the fuck are you doing? What are those kids up to now, Harry?' She could never bear to be away from him, always wanting it to be just them alone. As I've said, they were always at each other, pecking each other on the cheek, kissing, holding hands, and I thought that was disgusting. They were ancient, why on earth were they doing that? They weren't actually old, but when you're a kid, your parents seem about a hundred, so why in God's name were they up to that sort of thing? None of the other parents did that.

It wasn't all sunshine and lollipops for Rose either though, despite how she tried to frame it. I know that he did hit her on one occasion at least. There was a night when he came home after a few drinks and beat her so badly, he thought he'd killed her. He went to the cop shop in Ballymun and told them he'd murdered his wife. You couldn't make it up, but some other woman had been found dead that night and they thought he was talking about her. The Gardai hauled him over the coals working it all out, but nothing happened to him. When my Aunt Imelda saw Mom two weeks later, the marks were still on her face. That's the only time I've heard of him hitting her though – I don't think he would have had enough time to batter her as well as me and Alan. That kept him busy enough.

I think that, until I was four, my life was split. I had some happy times, I had Alan, I had my extended family, I had moments of laughter – but the other side was full of beatings, of hunger, of control. It was a very Jekyll and Hyde sort of life and I feel, at that point in my childhood, there was a fork in the road. There were two paths waiting for me but I wasn't the one who would be allowed to choose which one little Shaneda would be taken down.

He would do that for me.

CHAPTER 3

Princess

———

I'm now older and wiser, which makes me see the horror of what my life was about to become, but I do accept that when I was little, I adored my dad. I can also see that there were so many different dads within that one man. There was the Fun Dad, the Happy Dad, but there was also the Abusive Dad, who battered seven shades out of me so many times. I never looked at him as the same person with lots of personalities though, I separated them all out depending on who he was that day, or even in that moment.

My parents always had fancy things – Dad had a cine camera to make home movies, silent ones, and he would get me and Alan to roll down hills or do silly things. These are what give me good memories. He was always listening to music and I got my love of it from him, with his record player in the living room, the sounds of Debbie Harry and David Bowie and Cream filling the flat when he was in a good mood. Mom liked Patsy Cline and that would drone out whenever she chose what was to be played and she could never be encouraged to be more modern. She never really dressed like the other mothers her age, she always dressed older, and there wasn't a Fun Mom in the way there was a Fun Dad.

In fact, that green Elsie Tanner coat with the fur collar is the thing I associate most with how she looked for years when I was growing up. I once got separated from her in the local shopping centre and all I knew was that I had to look out for the coat. Finally, I saw it and rushed up to her, tugging at her sleeve and crying, 'Mom!' But it wasn't her, God knows how two women had been persuaded to buy that coat and walk around in it. When the other woman turned around and I saw it wasn't her, I swear I lost my life, thinking I'd never find her again. The woman took me to the cop shop that was just at the entrance to the shopping station and Mom turned up a few minutes later. The policewoman said to her, 'Is this your little girl, by any chance?' but she'd brought out some poor soul who had been there for three hours. They went back in and got me, and I never let that green coat out of my sight again when we went out.

Dad's music filling the house at weekends and him taking me and Alan out to photograph us are things which do still give me happy memories and thank God for the few there are. He used to develop his pictures in the bathroom as there were no windows in there, that was his darkroom. He took a lot of photos of Ballymun too, including ones from our seventh-floor window, where you could see the whole of the place and I remember some of them being really beautiful when it was all covered in snow. As he was in the Army, he kept fit, running a lot, going out with his towelling headband and tracksuit on. He had a lot of books on the Hollywood actor Arnold Schwarzenegger, a keen bodybuilder, and back in those days we all watched the TV wrestling with Big Daddy. The other telly event was when we watched *The Muppet Show*. I loved that, as did Alan, and we had the pyjamas to match the characters, which we always put on when we sat down to laugh at Kermit and his friends. There was a girl who sometimes babysat for us when our parents went out and after she'd put us to bed, she'd get me up again to watch *H.R. Pufnstuf* with her – those were safe, good times.

Dad was always doing something, he had lots of hobbies, but Mom did very little apart from knitting on a big, clanky machine. I don't think she had the same sort of world as Dad. He was working, interacting, whereas she had a smaller life which fitted in with her being a mousey person and staying in bed a lot, which I never worked out a reason for. Dad was very confident and more sociable, but she only had him.

It's very hard to know when abuse starts when you're so little. You don't know what it is, so you don't know what you're looking out for. It comes as a shock, but you're bewildered and don't have the words or even the sense of how to process it, which makes it very hard to say that it happened on a particular day at a particular time. I'm well aware that can be used against survivors – after all, if it was *that* bad, how can we not have a flashing red light in our memories? Surely we should know *that was the day, that was when it all began.* But life doesn't work like that and if people who want to diminish or deny what abused children go through, then that's their choice. We know. We can't forget the effects even if we don't know the specific day in some black calendar of terrible things.

I do firmly believe though that in the grooming process, abusers are aware that they'll be able to get away with it before they act on it. It's planned and it's something they have worked on for some time. The grooming isn't a separate thing, it's abuse too. My dad actually once asked me if I remembered the 'first time' – and this is part of how sick it all became – and he said, 'No, there was a time before that.' He remembered it even if I didn't.

A red-letter day for him, no doubt.

He told me that there was an occasion when I went into the bathroom when he was in the bath, something he had normalised for me and Alan, and he asked me to wash his chest. This wouldn't have bothered me; I was very little, maybe three years old, and all I was doing was playing with the bubbles on my dad. I saw something poking out of the water and asked him, 'What's that?'

'It's my willy,' he told me and then claimed that I started messing with it. He was also very clear at that point that he believed it was all my choice, that I'd started it and that it was perfectly fine. How in the world could a father believe that? A three-year-old child doing that? You'd tell her to stop, wouldn't you? Or never encourage her to start anything in the first place.

I guess you wouldn't if you were the sort of man he was.

I know the time that I thought it all began though. Not a date, not a day of the week, but the time that is first in my own mind. As I've said, I do think there would have been times before, but this one is there as *it*, as *that*.

I was lying on the leather sofa watching telly one night when I was about four years old. We were still in the Ballymun flat and this was a frequent set up. Dad was on the sofa first and he called me over to lie there with him, spooning, with him behind me as we cuddled up under a blanket. I don't remember what was on, but I do remember that all of a sudden, his hand was up my nightie and feeling inside my knickers. Touching my private parts, being somewhere he shouldn't be. I was never told, at that point or any other, that I needed to keep it secret; I was never threatened, it was just done. I have no memory of before or after, just of that happening, and we lay there on the sofa once he'd been down there in my knickers for a while. He was testing the waters, I'm sure of it.

We were in the Ballymun flat until I was seven and he touched me regularly after that initial time. He did it so often that I knew it would happen – to the extent, once when my Auntie Vivienne came to stay, I asked her to lie on the outside of my bed. I didn't tell her why, but I knew he wouldn't touch me in my bed if she was there. It became so normalised that I never felt fear, it was just something my dad did to me. I'd say that he did it pretty much any time I was on my own with him. I was very confused as a child because of it. He called me his 'Princess' and always had done, which made me think that when he touched me, it was something special between us, something only we did because he loved me so much and was showing me that love in that way. However, I couldn't understand why he still had those times when he got angry at me and Alan. If I was so special and we had our special thing together, why hadn't the battering stopped? I never verbalised that, but I did feel it – why was I special then, but not at other times?

Back then, the young ones, the teenagers, used to go round all the flats, selling newspapers so the tenants didn't have to bother going out for them. I spent a bit of time with one of those girls and one day, her boyfriend was there too. Once she'd sold her papers and the few bits from the shopping hut she'd been asked to get, the pair of them headed for the field. They sat down on the grass together while I was a little bit away from them and they started kissing. I remember very clearly thinking that I knew what they would do next because, by that time, I had already found pornography under Dad's bed. From those pictures, I knew what they were doing when they were lying in the grass and I fully expected them to move on to what I had seen. I don't know when I had first seen those magazines, but the images were there in my mind. Also, I don't know whether he had made sure I found them or even laid them out for me.

I might not have known what Dad was doing to me, but I had made the link. Also, I believe that my need to be as invisible as possible must have come from what he was doing to me. I didn't really ever want to be seen and that was why, when it was time to make my communion, I hated the idea and kicked up such a fuss. I felt like my communion dress would suffocate me and I began to dread the thought that I would have to go through the whole ceremony soon, probably choking as it happened. On the day, I was woken up and I started bawling, the very idea of people looking at me was terrifying.

'Get this dress on and stand still while I curl your hair,' Mom snapped at me. 'What are you moaning about anyway? Every other little girl does this, every other little girl knows it's special – why do you have to be different?'

'I don't want to go, I don't want to do it!' I kept saying, but she didn't care. It was going to happen, no matter how much I hated the idea. We weren't a particularly religious family, but this was important because it showed that we did the right things and as I've said, my parents always liked to be seen as that sort of family. I don't know what I thought the details of it were going to be, but when I walked back to my family, the texture of the wafer in my mouth made me want to gag and I was crying my eyes out. The priest had obviously been going on about the body of Christ and I had imagined the wafer would be something different, something nice, but it wasn't. I wanted to gawk (or gag). It didn't melt, it had gone into a horrific slime in my mouth and I couldn't believe they had given me such a thing. I wonder why that is – I wonder why I was gagging when all the other kids managed it.

At that time, I also started doing the strangest thing. I began stealing the rolls of film from the class projector. Corporal punishment was just being stopped in schools but our teacher still lined us up against the walls and slapped our hands with a ruler whenever anything went wrong. We all got that for the missing projector rolls which I had been taking home and hiding behind my wardrobe. Mom found them one day and I had to take them back, apologising to the teacher while still not knowing why I had even done it in the first place. Looking back, all of these things are clues, I guess – all of them are tiny indications that there was something very wrong going on in the world of that little girl – but no one was putting any of it together, even when I developed an eating disorder.

Food had always been an issue in our family. As I've said, Mom and Dad were more interested in buying the latest gadgets and shiny things to make them look good than putting food on the table. As I got older, there were more regular meals but I didn't want them. I used to hide food in the bin whenever Mom went out of the kitchen. I'd mush it up in my hands and stick it under the table or wash it under the tap until it was mashed enough to get down the plughole, but she never noticed. In fact, in later years, she said to me that teachers were always saying how fat I was. I've seen the pictures – I was as far from chubby as I could have been. I didn't want attention despite doing all of these things. It's as if there was a clash between the two different parts of what was going on.

When I was about six, Dad became a prison officer. Back then, you had to do a certain number of years to effectively be 'bought out'. Once he had done that, he was a security guard for a very brief time before moving to the prisons and he put in for a transfer from Dublin to Limerick. That meant we'd have to move. Mom and Dad went to visit a different house there while Alan and I stayed with our Aunt Liz for a few days and then we all moved there. The prison was only five minutes from our new house, but it wasn't available immediately so we were placed in prison accommodation. There were three rooms in one house, with all four of us in one of them and the other two used by two other prison officers. It had a sink and two beds. I don't even remember a little kitchen area, although the toilet was in another part of the house and we had to share it with those two other men so maybe the kitchen was in another part too.

On one of those few mornings when we lived there, Mom had taken Alan out as she often did. There was a library near to us and we would be taken there for books to pass the time, or to the little sweetie shop for a quarter of old-fashioned humbugs or apple drops. She would sometimes go with Alan on her own, as she had on this occasion, but never with just me.

'Princess!' Dad called over to me as I sat on my bed, playing. 'Come over here and give your dad a cuddle.' So, I did as I was told – I always did as I was told. I walked over and stood at the side of the bed, where he was covered by the blanket. I could see movement underneath the covers – he must have been masturbating, but I didn't know what that was then, and he started to touch me inside my knickers as he always did while I was standing there.

All of a sudden, the door opened and I saw a flash of one of the other men from the house. He must have opened our door by mistake and it was only for a split second, but that was the first time I felt fear of *me* getting into trouble, of *me* getting caught. I didn't think that Dad would be the one to get it in the neck, I thought it would be me. It was the first time I felt panic. That was how well I had been trained, I guess. That was the first time he had got me to stand by the side of the bed while he dealt with himself, but it was definitely the next stage and I knew that Mom wouldn't have found anything suspicious about him saying that she could leave me in the room while she went out with my little brother. I've often wondered if their close relationship was something that Dad encouraged so that he would have more access to me – everything was part of his grander scheme, I believe.

We were only in that accommodation for a couple of days before we rented another house up the road for the summer. In that house, Mom told us that she was pregnant again and I knew they were delighted by that as she'd lost a baby the year before. We were delighted too as I got a Sindy Doll, Alan got an Action Man and there was a chess set to share as part of the celebrations. I have no memory of my dad going near me in that house, that summer. I often wondered whether that was because he was happy about the new baby who was coming. Was he distracted, looking forward to this baby? In fact, he left me alone in the next house too, until the night Louise was born.

I only went to school for a little while in this house, but it was one run by nuns. We weren't strong Catholics, which meant that I didn't know a lot of the rules. One day, we were doing a prayer that obviously mentioned Jesus a lot of times. I could feel the eyes of one of the nuns staring at me throughout, boring into the very soul of me. I was completely oblivious to why she couldn't tear her eyes away until after it had finished.

'How dare you not bow your head every time you say Jesus!' she launched into me. 'How dare you! Who do you think you are? Who do you think you are, not showing respect to Jesus?' I'd never heard such a thing in my life. She was giving out to me, shaking me and getting herself into such a state. When I went home and told Dad what she had done, he went up to the school the next day and was roaring at her.

'Don't you ever put your hands on my daughter again!' he bellowed. 'You keep your hands off her, do you hear me? You keep your hands off her!' God, the irony. He could do whatever he wanted, but that nun wasn't allowed to even shake me. It's funny, looking back at the religious side of things, that Dad went in and out of it when it suited him. When Madonna's 'Like a Prayer' came out, you'd have thought he was the Pope. He was beyond offended by her burning a cross and the sacrilege of it all – I remembered that when I wanted to annoy him as a teenager and I painted black nail varnish over a cross on a necklace I had just to make him go mental. There were no religious pictures in the house though, we never had to pray to anything, it was just Mass every Sunday and that was all.

There was no rhyme nor reason to so much of it. The food, the beatings, the touching. I could never predict, I could never make sense of it. All I knew was that he loved me, that he loved his Princess, and I just had to wait and see which daddy I was going to get every day.

CHAPTER 4

Good Girl

———

We moved to our new house and I was becoming more and more anxious about little things. There was a teacher there called Mr O'Brien who had guinea pigs in the class. Every day, one of us was on the timetable to bring in carrots or parsnips for them. However, on the day it was my turn, Mom hadn't bothered to get anything and I remember it was breaking my heart all the way to school. I would get so worked up about little things, which was obviously a manifestation of just how toxic my home life was.

But I needn't have worried because Mr O'Brien was such a lovely man, but at times like that, I honestly thought I would collapse with worry. He was the one who started my love of reading. He got us to study Richard Adams' *Watership Down* and that was me from that point on.

I've never stopped with books really. He was a fantastic teacher and everything he did was an encouragement for me. I was a clever little girl, I just hated the attention that came if ever I put my hand up in class and was asked to speak in front of people. Dad was all for education too and used to like me to perform my reading, and we had been taught to write our names from an early age, with our Christmas stockings always having a lot of educational things in them. Mr O'Brien was by far the nicest teacher I had because in my next class in Limerick there was one who always made fun of my Dublin accent and I'd feel my face going red every time. When I was called Shanny rather than Shaneda, I knew it was a way of speaking that would be looked down upon in a lot of places. It was seen as common and I was on the alert that I had to be seen to fit in.

Mr O'Brien would never have done that, he would never have made fun of me. I knew that I did speak differently to them though – in Dublin, we'd say, 'You're massive!' but it means you're gorgeous. We say 'gas' when something is funny, we say 'ya' instead of 'yes' but we're not posh, and we say 'Mom' but we're not American. Having attention drawn to it was just something else to make me feel embarrassed though and dreading the attention which came from it.

Mom must have just been pregnant and no more when we moved into the new house as it was only September and my new sister came in the May of the following year. She made so many clothes for her and beautiful curtains hung from the ceiling around the cot. Louise was a planned baby and very much wanted.

The night she was born was one I'll never forget. I had just turned eight and came home from school one day to find only Dad there, making us corned beef toasties.

'What are you doing here?' I asked him.

'Your mom has gone into hospital to have the baby,' he told us and Alan looked at him with absolute terror in his eyes.

'What's wrong with you?' I snapped. 'What are you looking like that for?'

'Will Mom be OK?' he asked Dad.

'Of course she will, sure she's only having a baby,' he answered.

But Alan didn't look reassured at all.

'Is she going to die?' he wanted to know.

Dad sighed and I rolled my eyes while Alan continued to look as if his world was about to collapse. We all just went about our business until later that night. I was in my room when Dad shouted up to me, 'Where's Alan?' I had no idea, but it didn't take long to look through the house and work out that he had gone. He'd run away through sheer terror that Mom was going to die.

'Get in the car,' Dad said. 'We'll have to go find him.'

It was dark by then and we finally found him in an

estate where he should never have been, quite a distance from our house. He was dragged back home but there was just a feeling of relief that he'd been found. We both went to bed and I heard Dad going to his room too.

It wasn't long before he was calling for me. 'Shan, Shan, come here, will you?' It had been a fair time since he had done anything to me, but there was something in the tone of his voice that just made me hesitate for a moment before I went through. He was in bed, under the covers, in the dark – waiting for me, I suppose.

'Come in here, Princess,' he told me. 'Come here and be a good girl.'

I did as I was told – just like every other time. That was the first time I had been in a bed with him though, it had always been sofas before and it felt ominous – even though I wouldn't have known what that word was. It was just a feeling, a sense in my gut.

I was on my side with my back to him and he was touching me, as he always did, when, all of a sudden, I felt something warm and wet hit the side of my leg, at my thigh and on my back a little bit. It was hot and sticky and I wanted to wipe it off straight away – whatever it was, it was disgusting. He must have been prepared, he must have known he was going to do that on that night as he wiped me with a tissue that he just happened to have there.

'There you go,' he said casually, as if it was the most natural thing in the world to have ejaculated on your eight-year-old daughter. I went to the bathroom as there was still some of the disgusting stuff on me, then just went to bed. He had still never said to keep quiet, to keep this between us – he was so confident that I wouldn't say anything.

I wanted my mom but she wasn't there, she was having a baby while her husband spent the night abusing their firstborn.

Apart from that, I had a blissful summer. He must have just been trying it out, seeing if I would say anything, maybe checking whether I would tell Mom when she came back. It never even occurred to me though. She wasn't some sort of saviour in my world, whereas I loved my dad – I just wished he didn't do those horrible things.

I wandered all over that summer, out from morning till night, only going back for food – not that I could ever be sure I would get any as they used food as a means of control. I'd explore and have adventures, I don't even remember being hit for those couple of months. The summer before, I'd taught myself to ride a bike, getting myself an adult one from somewhere, just going up and down a hill, no matter how many times I fell off, until my legs did what they were meant to do, and I kept it up during those long, hot days too. There was a girl and boy who lived across the road and they had Atari games to play, which was the most brilliant thing, watching that little square hit from one side to the other. Another girl in a house behind us had a swing set, which I loved too. It was idyllic really. Alan and I spent a lot of time together and when we got on, we got on. However, when we didn't, we half killed each other – and we did it in silence. We'd have been battered again for battering each other.

I was actually very shy – I went to six different primary schools when I was a girl and all I ever did was follow Alan into them all as he was so confident. He'd stride in and make friends immediately, with me trailing behind him just hoping no one would notice me and that I could get through it all quite quietly. I remember having dolls and making clothes for them from scraps of material that Mom didn't use.

The main thing Alan and I used to love though is something that makes my blood run cold today. There was a railway track nearby and we liked nothing better than going down to it and pressing ourselves against the bushes as the trains sped past. It was the best thing in the world but we were really taking our lives into our hands every time we stood there, laughing and feeling the sheer thrill of it with the backwind in our faces and death brushing us inches away. I wasn't girly at all, I just wanted adventure and I was happiest when I was blending in, almost as a boy.

Mom and Dad started going out on a Saturday night after Louise was born, with a girl who lived in the house near the railway line coming over to babysit us all. I suppose it was their way of becoming the perfect couple again. We all wanted that ideal life in one way or another. For me, it was to have the Nice Dad rather than any of his other personalities.

I adored my dad and wanted to be a prison officer just like him.

'No, Shanny,' he would say to me. 'It takes a certain type of person, someone with no heart, and that's not you.' He'd say stuff like that and it means more now as I go back and unpack it all.

Everyone loved him. If he was out the front of the house, the neighbours would all talk to him, he was seen as such a great guy. Everybody loved Harry and he commanded respect because of his job. It's so often the case with abusers, they hide behind that façade of respectability and everyone is fooled, because they're all being groomed too.

There was one neighbour who took a shine to me rather than him though, an old woman called Ena. I recall very clearly that there was one day that Mom was painting the bathroom and even though she was still pregnant with Louise at that point, she climbed up onto the toilet seat to reach the ceiling. She slipped off but for some reason, Dad came to find me and beat the shit out of me for it happening even though it wasn't my fault in the slightest and I'd been downstairs at the time.

'Why the fuck did you do that?' he yelled.

'Do what?'

'Let your mother hurt herself?'

'I wasn't even there,' I told him. 'I wasn't even in the room.'

'Like I fucking care!' he replied.

That was the truth actually – he didn't care, he just liked to hit us.

Ena often asked me to walk to the shops with her and the next time I saw her, she said, 'I heard you crying – were you OK?'

'Yeah,' I told her. 'I fell off the bottom step.'

I'd never been told to say anything or lie when we were asked anything. Ena bought me some marigolds after that and even gave me a window box to grow my own. When I think of her now, she must have heard so much through those walls. Could she have said anything, could she have done anything? I don't know, I certainly don't blame her. She showed me little kindnesses and that meant a lot.

Obviously, Dad would never have stopped. Abusers don't, unless they're caught and who was going to catch him? The only time anyone had come close to seeing what he did was when that man accidentally walked into the room and it was me who was terrified, not my father. It was progression, I see that now – from the sofa, from touching me there, to the bed where he had ejaculated over me in a planned way because he had that tissue ready. Baby steps, but never ones that would go backwards.

One day, when Mom was out with Louise, he called to me: 'Shan! Princess! Come here, will you? I need you.'

I just knew. There was nothing, *nothing*, that he 'needed' me there for. He was in his bedroom, I knew from the direction of his voice.

'What is it? What do you want?' I shouted back, trying to buy time, trying to see if I could get out of this.

'I told you – come here.'

I squeezed my eyes tight and took a deep breath. Maybe I was wrong. Maybe I had done something that had made him angry – maybe I would just be getting battered. How awful to wish for that, but the alternative was a lot worse. Anyway, he had called me 'Princess'. He only did that when he was being nice. *His* version of nice.

'Shan – get here NOW!'

I couldn't delay it any longer. Opening my eyes, I told myself I could get through whatever he was going to do. He was usually quick when he touched me on the sofa and he was definitely quick that time all the hot, sticky stuff had landed on me. Walking into his room, I saw him lying on the bed, on his side.

He patted the mattress. 'There you are. Good girl, come here.'

A child just doesn't have any power in that moment. I didn't even have the words for what he had been doing, so how could I have made a case to him that I didn't want to do anything at all? I certainly didn't want to lie down beside him, but he was my dad and I was just a little girl.

There wasn't far between the door and his bed. In a few steps, I was there. He patted the mattress again and I lay down on my back. He turned me away from him with my back pressing into the front of his body, pushed my dress up from my legs and I felt it – I felt that thing, hard, pressing into my back. He started touching me, his hands and fingers getting quicker and quicker as I stared at a spot on the wall, willing it to be over and also dreading that it would happen again.

It did.

The horrible, hot, gooey thing was all over me again, over my legs and back, and I could smell it. I didn't know what it was, I couldn't have described it, but it is the smell of a man that I hate to this day.

'Good girl. Good girl, Princess,' he said and I was handed a tissue again. He rolled onto his back and I leapt up, rushing to the bathroom, rubbing at my sticky skin with soap and water. That was the next stage. That was what he had groomed me to do, and as I had known in my heart of hearts, there would be no going back – there would only be more horror to come.

CHAPTER 5

Normal

—

In that house, a horrible pattern developed of Dad regularly masturbating while he touched me and ejaculating over my back and legs. I suppose he must have been working out how much he could get away with and it was always a case of ramping it up. Perhaps I should have known that the next stage would be for me to touch him but I never thought ahead, I never anticipated how much worse it could become.

The first time he wanted me to do that, to touch him there, he tried to make it seem as if it was an interesting experiment.

'Touch that and see if you can make it grow,' he suggested as if it was a game. There was always just an assumption that I would do it and he was right – I did.

He showed me how to move my hands up and down but would get annoyed because they were little and I would get tired and sore.

'I can't do it any more,' I'd tell him. 'It hurts too much.'

'No, no, it doesn't, Princess. Keep going, keep going,' he'd coax. I was used to obeying him and had tried to this time, but what was happening now was something beyond what I had done in the past. This was agony.

'It does, Dad, it hurts.'

'Just keep trying, Princess, just keep trying. You can do it, I know you can.'

You'd have thought he was encouraging me to stick with my spelling or arithmetic. He was oblivious to the fact that I hated it, that it hurt me, that I didn't want anything to do with this horrible thing he had decided we had to do together. All that mattered to him was that he was getting what he wanted. He was getting bolder with it all and it felt as if he thought he was never going to get caught.

Alan was going to Scouts by this time and Dad would always get me to go with him in the car when it was pick-up time.

'Come on, Shan,' he would shout, keys jangling in his hand, 'let's get that brother of yours.' I did want to be with him, I did want Nice Dad, but I had this constant feeling in my gut that he wanted the other thing from me. I just wanted to be his Princess with no strings attached.

One night, we were in the car waiting outside the Scout Hall for my brother and I was on the seat next to Dad.

'Touch it,' he told me.

I looked at him, shocked. 'Touch it here?'

'Yes. Go on, touch it. Do it for me,' he begged.

'Dad, we're outside. Anyone could see.'

'No, we're not. Not really. Who's going to look in the car? They're just picking their kids up. Go on, Princess. Go on.'

What could I do? I had to try. Now that he had trained me to masturbate him, he knew it could be done – and, from everything I had seen, once he knew something could be done, that was what he wanted all the time. So, that became his next habit, him wanting me to masturbate him while we waited for Alan. Every little thing that afforded him access to me was something that was used to abuse – being alone in the house, collecting Alan, lying on the sofa watching TV, all of it was turned into something nasty.

And all of it was empowering him – he must have been feeling invincible. One evening, at the weekend, we were all watching TV together. Dad was on the couch with Mom, snuggling into each other and being all smoochy as usual. Alan and I had one eye on the telly, one eye on annoying each other, while Louise was asleep in her cot. It was a normal family scene – in fact, it probably looked quite loving if you'd seen it from the outside. I was shoving

Alan about and he was giving as good as he got, when I noticed Dad unwrap himself from Mom.

'Just going upstairs for something,' he told her, casually.

She settled herself into the cushions and turned the telly up as he left the room, smiling at me as he went past. Within minutes, I heard his voice from upstairs.

'Shan, come here!'

I ignored him, concentrating as hard as I could on the TV.

'Shan! Shan!'

Don't answer, I told myself, *don't react. Don't go.*

'Shaneda, can you not hear your father calling on you?' said Mom.

'Nope.'

'Well, he is! Get upstairs now.'

'I don't want to.'

'Don't be so cheeky! Go on, get up there.'

Trudging upstairs, I could hear her and Alan in the living room, a normal family night. Surely Dad couldn't really be wanting me to do the thing with all of them in the house, with all of them knowing that he was alone with me when there was no real reason for that to be the case? As soon as I approached his open bedroom door, I realised that was exactly what he was expecting. Lying on his bed as usual, patting the mattress beside him again.

'You took your time,' was all he said before it began.

Again, I was terrified that it would be me who was

found out and that I would be the one who would get in trouble. It became a common occurrence, our *new* common occurrence. Mom would be downstairs watching TV while Dad went upstairs and only a few minutes later would call on me to come up and do those things. I always knew what he was leading up to now, I knew that he wanted the sticky stuff to come out of him. He never told me I was a good girl. He'd give me a hug and then I'd leave the room, or we'd go home with Alan in the car if it was during a Scouts pick up.

From the time the man in the prison officer accommodation had opened the door on us and I'd been so ashamed that I was going to get caught, I did have that sense of knowing I would be embarrassed if anyone knew about this, but I also had the thought that it happened to other little girls too. The reason I thought this was because of Amy, a friend I had made at some point, although I can't remember how or when. My memory is a bit like that – I have a mind like a steel trap for so much, but innocuous things like when I met a little girl who would be a friend just disappear into the mist.

Amy and I spent a lot of time together and one day she said to me, 'My daddy touches me, does yours?'

It was as straightforward as that, but we both knew what she meant. We both knew where and we both knew that it was something we didn't want.

I nodded.

'In my knickers,' Amy confirmed, a statement, not a question.

I nodded again. 'Me too.'

'You know, Shaneda,' she continued, 'I don't think it's very nice and I don't think I want him to do it any more.'

'It's not very nice, Amy,' I agreed. 'It's not very nice at all. Does your daddy make you touch his willy too?'

'He does, he does indeed.'

We spoke about it a few times after that, but not in a way that you would say we were dwelling on it. These things our daddies did were just facts and if Amy's did that to her, and mine did that to me, maybe it was something that happened a lot more than I had ever thought.

'We should run away,' I said to her one day as we sat in the park.

'We should, you're right, we should!' She was very enthusiastic about it – and why wouldn't she be? We both had something that needed to stop, but if the daddies doing it couldn't see that, we'd have to take action.

'How would we get things though?' I asked her. 'Food and sweets and stuff that we'd need?'

We ran our toes through the grass as we thought about it. We definitely needed to leave, but until we made our fabulous new life, we would probably have to cover ourselves.

'I reckon we need a ten-pound note,' Amy said wisely. 'We need a packet of Taytos and an ice freeze a day, and the money would do it for a while, then we'll find a family that will let us live with them. A *nice* family,' she emphasised.

'Do you think those people we see down by the railway track would take us?' I asked her. We were always watching them from the trees and they only lived about half a mile away. We didn't really have any idea what they were like, but if we were making up a fantasy life, why not include them?

'Deffo,' Amy answered, nodding her head. 'That's the plan, don't you think?'

'Sure, but where will we get TEN POUNDS?' I gasped.

'I'm not sure, but the first one of us to get it is a sign. It doesn't matter if it's me or it's you. Soon as we have it, we go. Deal?'

I nodded gravely. This seemed like a grand plan and there was absolutely nothing that could go wrong with it. We'd get the money, we'd run away, we'd get taken in by the lovely family and everything would be perfect. I was sure that Amy would get the ten pounds before me, so I waited for a few days until, would you believe it, Mom handed me one with a list.

'Get yourself down to the shop for this,' she said. 'And don't take long, just there and back.'

I looked at the ten pounds and the list of shopping she needed and my heart flew. I had the ten pounds, I had the ten pounds! Now all I needed was Amy. Our new life was waiting for us. I ran to her house and found her outside, playing.

'Amy, look,' I whispered, even though there was no one to hear us – or care. She gasped as I pulled the crumpled tenner out of my pocket and, speaking just as quietly, said, 'Shaneda, that's it – we need to go. Now!'

Without any more thought, the pair of us fled down towards the railway track. I threw the folded-up shopping list into a bush and then started to scramble across the tracks. Somehow, I lost my footing, even though I'd made that trip so many times in the past. I fell and smacked my face off a wooden beam and when I got up, I couldn't see properly.

Amy had got across safely and I shouted to her, 'Everything's gone a bit funny, it's all kind of fuzzy!' I was staggering about and we both decided that maybe that day wasn't the best one for running away. I got home, everything spinning around me, with a lump hanging out of my head. Mom was watching telly when I got in and started roaring at me immediately.

'Where's my stuff? Where's my fags? Where's my sugar? Have you got any of it?'

'I fell, Mom,' I told her. 'I'm really not feeling quite right.'

'Like I care!' she screamed. 'Get back and get it, now!'

And I did – I went to the shop for everything she needed, then traipsed home again. As soon as I got in the door,

I began vomiting everywhere and she suddenly realised I was hurt, putting a wet towel on my forehead. That was my first attempt at running away but it wouldn't be my last. Amy and I never discussed doing it again. I guess we'd tried, but it hadn't worked, or maybe we'd never thought we would get to that stage in the first place and the possibility of it had shocked us.

We were both right back into the abuse we had to endure. I liked spending time with Amy, but what we had shared hung heavy between us – not the running away, that could just be rewritten as something kids do, or at least plan to do, but the fact that we both had horror shows at home.

I did spend some time at her house and used to love being on the swing set in her back garden. We would talk about school and the other kids, toys and sweets, but that undercurrent was there. One afternoon during summer, her dad came out to join us and we sat on the swing seat with him in between us both. Just another father spending time with his little girl, just another good dad. He put his arm around me and it went a little higher than it should, then a little lower than it should, cuddling me in a sleazy way – and I knew. I knew what those hands did to my friend because similar hands were doing just the same to me in a house not far away.

CHAPTER 6

Bath Night

———

By that stage, Dad was making me touch him a couple of times a week. It was my normality in that house for about two years, from when I was seven until I was nine. One thing that did become clear to me was that my parents felt completely differently towards my baby sister Louise than to me and Alan and treated her differently too. She would get treats, such as skinny Milky Bars every day, whereas we'd be told we were too old for sweets. Louise was the golden child, that's for sure – I couldn't understand why she was so loved and I wasn't. I fully admit that I resented her.

We moved to Mom's parents in Kildare for the summer when I was nine while Dad stayed in Limerick. They had decided to buy a house there rather than rent and he was getting everything in order for that to happen. He came to visit us every weekend and it was in that house, the house of my grandparents, that I started to wonder about how much my mom knew of the abuse and to what extent she was colluding with it. The house was a three-storey one with just a single bedroom on the top floor, which was for Mom, Alan, Louise and me, with Dad staying there too on his weekend visits. The stairs up to that room were creepy and creaky, and it was such a trek from the ground floor, where the kitchen and sitting room were.

Dad would stay in bed while the rest of us got up in the morning, so the first time Mom said that I was to bring a cup of tea up to him, I thought nothing of it other than I hated those stairs. Rushing up them as quickly as I could while balancing the mug of hot tea, I walked in that first time Mom told me to take it to him and he was lying there, masturbating in bed.

'Come here and stand beside me,' he told me.

Trying to distract him, I said, 'I've brought you your tea.'

'Very good, but come here, Princess.'

'I don't want to.'

'Yes, you do. You *do* want to.'

It was just as it always was. Me standing at the side of the bed while he touched me with one hand and himself with the other. I remember that the door to the room was never closed – he was so sure he wouldn't be disturbed and

I think that was one of the things that made me wonder about Mom. That summer, he seemed to do it all the time. It was a beautiful summer, the sun was always streaming in, and I would just try and concentrate on that while he made me touch him or helped himself to touching me. He must have felt invincible with that door open all the time, Mom telling me to bring him tea two or three times a day and no one saying a word. As well as my grandparents, there were three of my uncles and their wives staying there at that time, with not a single one of them bothering or noticing that a nine-year-old child was being abused under their roof.

In the village was a tiny chemist and a Post Office as well as a little shop that was almost a boutique. After Mom started getting me to bring cups of tea to Dad, with all that entailed, he would take me out on the Saturday, into the village, and ask me if I wanted anything. It wasn't long before I realised this was my payment. I could have the sweets he never otherwise gave me, I could have comics – I could have anything I asked for as long as I did those things he wanted.

One week, I noticed a jumper in the boutique window and my eyes popped out of my head. It was at the time when BMX bikes were all the rage and this glorious article was baby pink with the logo across it. *Well, if I have to do what he wants, at least I'll get as much out of it as I can*, I thought. I had been asking for more and more, escalating it, and that seems such a terrible thing now. I got earrings, a ring with a ladybird on it, anything I wanted, but even now, that BMX jumper was a symbol of how things were becoming, that he was making me feel that it was a trade.

I felt a huge sense of relief when he left every Sunday, but as the week went on, I knew he'd be back soon. There was a feeling of dread in my stomach as the days passed, although at other times I had a lot of fun. Alan and I played in the bog – which maybe doesn't sound great, but it was for us then. He used to jump off from high parts over the dip in the bog where all the water collected and I was so scared he would hurt himself but he never did. We'd go collecting mushrooms with our uncle too and it's only now that I understand why he wanted them so much and what type of mushrooms they were!

We were in that house for about two months, from the end of June through all of the summer. It was like Groundhog Day – Dad abusing me all through the weekends and Mom ignoring me most of the time. We moved so much that I never really had friends and after that one little girl who was being abused too, Amy, there was no one who gave me a sense of what other families were like.

The next house we lived in was in a tiny village in County Clare called O'Callaghan's Mills. I hated the place from the moment I set eyes on it. My parents were meant to be buying the house from another prison officer and we all moved in while the sale was being put through – it was the reason we had been living with Nanny Rooney to begin with. We were there for about eight months although they never did buy it as the place was falling apart (literally – one of the walls collapsed onto the street after a few months). I felt like we were living in hillbilly land and the sound of the banjos would have followed me to my grave if I had to stay there forever. I was only nine but I felt like I could have won *Mastermind* there compared to everyone else. Backwards was putting it mildly. It was a real way of country living that I'd never experienced before and I wanted no part of it.

After about a week, Mom bought my brother and me wellies, which made me bawl my eyes out as I thought it meant I would be there forever now that I had the uniform. 'I don't want to be a farmer!' I screamed. 'Don't make me be a farmer!'

Coming from a big city to a twelve-house place where everyone knew each other and said hello on first name terms was not what I wanted. On more than one occasion, there was a cow in our garden and farmers were always tracking down animals that had wandered away. School was a rickety old building without enough kids to justify having separate year groups. In mine, there were only ten kids spread across two years and I think most of them were related to each other. They all seemed to know each other outside school. It was a close family community I suppose.

It's the first time I felt complete and utter sadness, and a lot of that was because of where we were living. It was all so old-fashioned as the girls were taught to sew and the boys had football lessons. I wanted more than that.

In that house, I really started noticing the way my brother and I were treated compared to our little sister. Louise would only have been one but it was like night and day. We used to get logs delivered to the house and I'd be out there, trying to break them up with an axe for them to go into the range, while she was inside being looked after like the most precious child in the world.

'You've done well there,' Dad told us one day. 'Choose one each and take them inside.'

Confused, Alan and I looked at each other.

'Choose what?' I asked.

'One each.'

I was still puzzled. 'One what?'

'A log, take a log each.'

We knew better than to question him but had no idea why he'd think we wanted a bloody log each. So, in we traipsed, only for Dad to tell us, 'There you go, there are your new seats.' It was weird, mind-messing stuff like that, which meant we never knew how we'd be treated from one day to the next.

It was in that house where I was in the bath one day when he came in to wash my hair out. I was still quite young, only nine, and although I was trusted to clean myself, it was harder to do my long hair. I did try though. I'd just lathered up the shampoo when Dad came into the room.

'I'll help you with that,' he said.

'No, it's fine, I can do it,' I told him. I wasn't just saying that as a child trying to learn how to do things for themselves, I was saying it to get him out of there. I didn't want him to see me naked and there was something about him being in such a closed, private space with me that screamed danger.

'Don't be stupid, tip your head back.'

I did as I was told. We always kept a plastic jug at the side of the bath for washing our hair and he dipped it in the water, then poured. The soapy suds washed down into my face more than anything as he dipped the jug in again to get the last remnants of shampoo. As he did so, I felt the most excruciating pain shoot through my private parts. Dear God, I'd never felt agony like it. While Dad had been rinsing my hair with one hand, he had been pushing the fingers of his other into me.

I was roaring and crying, so loud that time as I thought I was going to die from the agony. This was something I couldn't keep quiet about, this wasn't him touching himself or touching me in the way he had done before, this was absolute torture. It even made Mom come into the hall.

'What's wrong with her?' she shouted.

'She got shampoo in her eyes,' Dad replied. 'Nothing

to worry about – she's just moaning about it.' He was totally calm though. There was never any sense of him worrying that he might be found out. And there was never an apology. Ever. Mom didn't even bother to come and see what was going on in the bathroom, she just walked away.

I don't remember getting out of the bath or him saying anything to me. What I do recall is that it felt he had ripped something open. I went to my room in complete terror – he had done something so bad, something that had hurt me in a way I had never even imagined. Although everything else had been awful, this … this was incomprehensible.

For the next few days, I was terrified. What if he started trying that when we were on the sofa or when he called me? He didn't, but the next time I had a bath, I knew I had to check what he had done. I could feel a hoop of skin hanging as if a piece of – what I know now is – my hymen had been partially opened. I always thought it was like when you push the foil on a pint of milk and there is only a bit of it that comes away. That was me, that was what he did to me.

As I'd suspected, it became the norm for him to touch me like that. When I brought him his cup of tea and was standing at the side of bed, in his fingers would go – once he did something, there was never any going back. He was always adding on a bit extra. The fact that the new house was a bungalow and yet I was still being told to bring him those cups of tea showed how supreme he was, king of the castle. Mom didn't work, she didn't drive, but that never stopped him – he was quite happy to abuse me when she was there as he knew she couldn't care less about us being alone together for no real reason.

What people will find hard to understand was that I still loved him. The moments when he was Nice Dad, the moments when he was kind and encouraging, were all that kept me going. I thought that if I did the right thing, if I managed to be the right sort of little girl, he would stop the other stuff. I don't think I ever thought that Mom finding out would stop it – I thought she would blame me, that I would get called names. For a child to grow up in that sort of environment, with so many things upside down, makes them hold onto any sort of emotion and love. A lot of us have more understanding of grooming now. I was groomed to within an inch of my life and that was abuse from the moment it began. Everything had built up – the sofa touching, the pornography, the bringing him cups of tea, the way he masturbated on me, the way he taught me to masturbate him, the abuse in the car when we collected Alan or went on any other sort of trip together, the abuse in the bath, every single aspect was a way in which he accumulated control.

And then the other parts – the frequent beatings, which were always unpredictable unless Mom had asked for them, the lack of love from her, the way in which they both treated Louise differently, the withholding of food until they decided to feed us, the constant moving from one house to another. It was like being in a cult, never knowing from one moment to another what would be thrown at me – the only constant was the abuse. There was scarcely a day when Dad didn't touch me. He always managed to find a moment, find a time when his hands would be at me. I dreaded Mom telling me to bring him a cup of tea, I dreaded bathtime. I dreaded him being in his bed, I dreaded me being in my bed. I dreaded watching TV in case I was asked to cuddle him on the sofa. I dreaded it all – but it was only just beginning ...

CHAPTER 7

Presents

———

That was the first Christmas that he asked for his present from me, which was to have a good old feel and wank while I stood there, saying nothing. That Christmas, in 1984, I was given a green jewellery box with a cross stitch on top that you could do yourself. It was a little panda bear, I'll always remember that. I also got a glass bead jewellery kit. That Christmas night, while everyone was in the living room watching telly, he called to me from his bedroom, where he was watching something too. It would have been some sort of Chuck Norris or Bruce Lee film, he liked all that macho shite and was obsessed with Arnold Schwarzenegger, so it could have been any of them.

'Where's my Christmas treat?' he asked.

'I don't have any presents to give you.'

'Sure you do.'

'I really don't, Dad, I don't have anything.'

'You've always got something for me, Princess – go on, give me my Christmas treat.'

I thought I might get away with it because of it being Christmas, but no such luck. I stood there, stitching the jewellery box, actually stitching it, watching the panda come to life and saying nothing while he went on with what he was doing.

That was the first time I know I dissociated from what was being done to me. Christmas and birthdays should have been my happy days but he ruined them all. I think back to my twelfth birthday when he gave me a swimsuit, ostensibly so that we could go swimming together and he could teach me to become good at it. As soon as we started, as soon as we got in, his fingers were in me, under the water. It didn't matter that we were surrounded by other people, he knew I wouldn't say anything. To this day, it's all I think about when someone asks me why I don't swim. That's why – that's why.

That was the first Christmas that he asked for his present from me, which was to have a good old feel and wank while I stood there, saying nothing. Every time it was my birthday, I would ask him if it could stop – I was getting too old (as if that was the point). He would always agree but the next day, he'd be back at me again.

Going back to Christmas, there weren't lavish piles of gifts but there was always something we wanted in what we did get. I had that box for years and I do have some good memories even though the horror runs through it all. We never used to have junk food in the press on ordinary days and we were certainly never allowed to just help ourselves to anything, but at Christmas, all that changed. All the minerals were bought, Lilt, Fanta, an endless supply of sweets and Taytos, Scots Clan toffee, big tins of Roses and Quality Street, and you didn't have to ask, you could freely go and take anything. Tubes of Smarties and Jelly Tots, little boxes of sweets, big bags of crisps, all of it, filling the press in the kitchen in a wonderful free-for-all which definitely made me look forward to the holiday in that sense. There was no obsessive Church presence for us – we did go to one service in Hicksville, but apart from the odd Communion, it wasn't part of my life. No midnight Mass or anything like that.

I think abusers do choose women who will go along with it a lot of the time – they target them. Abuse can happen to anyone, at any stage of life, but I feel that abusers do have a radar – they develop the vulnerability of their victims too. They isolate and divide, they often love bomb just to make you feel there is something you can do to get the good feelings back when it turns sour, they make you feel that no one will believe you and they are often seen as great people by their families and communities.

Paedophiles, not men who do it in the moment, are clever people, masters of what they do. When I had kids, if someone was upstairs with one of my kids, even their dad, I would be up there to see if everything was OK. Normal people do that, good people do that, but I was just left with him on so many occasions and my mom turned a blind eye at best, but maybe she colluded with it – I do wonder about that when I think of all the times she told me to bring him a cup of tea especially. These men know exactly what to do. If they put their energies into something else, they would take over the world. They own your mind, body and soul, and that's worse than the actual sexual abuse at times. Afterwards, as a woman, the fact that they are in your head is the worst thing.

He had me brainwashed that the guards (police) were scum and I should never tell them anything. One day he was stopped and they asked him what his name was. He refused to tell them.

'What do you want my name for? What business is it of yours?' He went on and on until eventually one of the cops said, 'Come on Mr Daly, no need to be like that.'

'So, you know my fucking name!' he shouted. With that, he left, ranting and raving at us.

'You never have to tell them your fucking name, do you hear me? Never tell them a fucking thing, never trust them.' It was us against them which made it even more unlikely that I would disclose. Everything makes sense now, why he would want me to think that way and why he was pleased if I disrespected the guards.

Afterwards, after the abuse, he would always say, 'Go on now, get back to your mom,' and that would be my signal that he was done with me ... Until the next time. I would head back to the rest of the family, who had been going on with life as usual. There were amazing Christmas films on every year and they would be watching them whereas I had this blip in the middle that was part of my normality.

He taught me how to play chess in that house.

'I'm brilliant at this,' he told me. 'Just watch. I'll teach you as we go, you'll never win but you should look at how good I am.'

I think it took three games before I beat him and he refused to play with me after that. He upturned the board in anger and I was shocked – not at that, but at the fact I had beaten him. Sure, wasn't he the smartest person in the world? He was always telling me that, but if I'd won, what did that make me? He had to be the best at everything – well, at least he had to claim he was, but he was a mediocre man who got his pleasure from abusing a little girl. Not much to be proud of, was it?

I was quite young when I realised that I could irritate him if I wanted to. He would go mental, screaming, as he liked to be the big man in every situation. I would get brazen but it was baby steps at that point, like the chess.

We moved to the next house when I was just about to turn ten, this one was in Raheen in Limerick. It seemed the same as a lot of the others: three bedrooms, semi-detached, nothing to write home about and nothing which signposted the horrors that were happening within. It was maybe a bit nicer than the others and there were other kids around. Alan made friends easily and I kept up my habit of following my brother, even though he was younger, in the hope that I would meet some people too. I relied on him as he had this confidence I lacked. I was a very shy, held-back sort of child, all I did was survive and that was enough. Mom got a job as a hospital cleaner at this point, the first one I could remember, which meant that Dad had even more access to me.

There was a time in that place, when I was still ten, and my brother and I went to an estate where they were building houses in a fenced part. There were only two of them half-built so far. The builders, foolishly, left all the front and back keys in the locks every night when they went home and we raced up to the attic of one of them as soon as we found out. The floor fell through and I ended up with concussion. I remembered so little but it did give me an idea – I put it in my memory bank for when I might need it.

This was the house where I first ran away on my own. My dad had been in work one day and when he came home, he asked me to clean his car with my brother. I didn't do it to his liking and his hand flew across my face while he looked at it and then punched me in the head.

'Get to the shop and get out of my sight,' he snarled at me. 'Milk. Bread. Sausages. Now!'

I took off on my bike as soon as he threw the money at me. Vicious attacks were always on the cards when he was in a bad mood, you just didn't know at what point or how bad they would be. He'd be enraged usually, grinding his teeth. This one had left my head ringing and I'd had enough. If he'd hit me that hard in the street, God knows what it would be like when he got me inside. I was cycling around for about an hour before the wheel of my bike went over something. I fell off and hit my head. Lying in the street, a couple found me and asked my name so that they could get me home.

'I don't know,' I told them. 'I don't know my name!'

It came to me in a flash – if I didn't know who I was, then I couldn't be taken back and my parents wouldn't be able to find me. I'd feign concussion and all would be well.

'Let's get you to hospital then,' the woman said. 'You poor thing, that must have been some clatter to your head.'

I felt quite pleased with myself as they drove me to the hospital – but when the nurse took my coat off, she found a note inside.

'Oh, look at this,' she said. 'It's a note to school from your mother!' My heart sank. She'd written that only the week before and I hadn't handed it in. On it, clear as day was my name – and hers. 'Rose Daly,' the nurse read out.

'We've got a cleaner working here of that very name. I'll give her a ring and see if she's your mum.'

I was a bit out of it with my head injury but I do remember that when my parents turned up, the guards were there and got them in a bit of trouble for not reporting me missing as it was dark by that point. I still pretended that I didn't know who I was, but it was a lost cause. I saw Dad walking towards me after the guards were finished with them and all I could think was, *oh shit*. I kept up the pretence of not knowing my name but it was clear they were my mom and dad, so I was dragged home. I'd run away, he didn't have his food and the guards had been at him, so I knew I would get it.

I wasn't very lucky on that bike as I fell off another time, fracturing the back of my arm. I went to the hospital and told them Mom worked there and they put a cast on. When she collected me, I just knew that Dad would go mad when I got in – but he didn't. There was no predicting what he would do.

The next fall saw me hurt my legs so badly, I needed crutches.

'Now, that ankle is badly broken,' the nurse told me. 'You need to be careful or it won't set properly. Rest it when you can and rely on the crutches whenever you're walking about. They're there to help you, don't think you can do without them, OK?'

I nodded my agreement. I really was always getting into

scrapes but this time I'd be careful. I was out of the house a lot – who wouldn't be? – and my bike was my pride and joy. It was proving to be quite unlucky though.

'We'll take good care of her,' Dad promised, then drove me home. As I sat in the back of the car, I was in a lot of pain and he hadn't told me to get in the front, which came as a great relief as it meant that I wasn't going to have to wank him off in the hospital car park as well as deal with my ankle.

It was night-time when we got home and I hobbled into the hallway of the house with the lights still off, the place almost in darkness. I don't know where Mom and Alan were – they might just have been in another room, keeping themselves to themselves although it is odd that a mother wouldn't come out to see how her daughter was after a trip to hospital.

I was barely in the door before Dad kicked the crutches away from me. There was no talk, just a vicious battering as I stood there, crouched there, fell there, my ankle in agony and the pain ripping through me. I think he got a huge amount of pleasure from being so unpredictable. My hatred for him really started that night. I might not have known much, but I knew that wasn't the normal reaction of a parent to their child's broken ankle.

I've often wondered whether Dad's anger and reaction to me getting into trouble or being in hospital was coloured by some worry that I might disclose the abuse. Any time I went to the doctor or was in hospital, he would be there, bringing me what I needed, bringing me to appointments. Mom didn't drive at that point, but she never even tried to come – did he tell her not to? He would always appear from work and I'm sure he looked great, he looked like the doting father.

Around that time, I was standing at the top of the stairs one day, swaying, thinking, *if I throw myself down, will it kill me?* I just wanted to be dead. By that point, I knew the words, I knew I had been sexually abused, but I don't know how I knew. Back then, we didn't have *EastEnders* or any other TV programmes like that where I might have learned from the storylines and it wasn't spoken about, so how I knew I have no idea. There was part of my mind thinking, *yes, I think it'll kill me and I want that*, but there was another part saying, *what if it doesn't?*

I knew it wasn't foolproof, there was a chance that I would throw myself down and I'd be facing broken limbs or even paralysis. I'd get no comfort from my parents if that happened. Without a guarantee of death, I couldn't do it. I would have to keep living my life of torture until I could find the strength – or the promise – of an escape from it all.

CHAPTER 8

House of Doom

That house in Raheen was where the abuse really escalated. I can't give a neat order, a neat line of dates, but I do know that house was where I was introduced to porn on a much more regular basis. The video player had a remote control but it was still attached to a lead that went to the machine itself. It was, I suppose, 'normal' porn. There were no animals, nothing like snuff movies, no torture, no anal, no choking – all the stuff that is so accessible and normalised now. The films I was shown were men and women doing things that I had no idea about, things that I couldn't really comprehend – especially when the women put the men's things in their mouths. *Why would they do that?* I wondered, from the start. *Why would you put a fella's mickey in your mouth?* But I didn't have to wonder for long. Dad was showing me these films as an instruction manual and it was almost immediately that he wanted me to do what I'd seen.

The room had the blinds closed and was dark, he was sitting beside me on the horrible squeaky sofa we had, the one I had started to associate with it all. His arm would come around me before he started wanking himself off and touching me. Louise and Alan would be in bed – she was only small and would be asleep anyway if Mom was at work and Alan wouldn't have dared raise a word to Dad, even if he was sending him to bed when it was still light outside. It had to be just us, it had to be just him and his Princess.

I got a running commentary.

'That's a blow job,' he told me as if we were watching a fecking David Attenborough programme. 'Go on, you give it a go.'

'You want me to do THAT?' I said, horrified. 'You want me to put your lad in my mouth?'

'Go on, Princess, just give it a go. Let's try it. Everyone does it, you'll like it,' he tried to reassure me.

'I will not like it,' I told him, but he was insistent – I had to try. I was trying not to be sick but the taste of it, the pressure of it wasn't something I could get past. I pulled back from it and said, 'No! No, Dad, I can't do it.' It hadn't worked out as the sordid little fantasy he'd hoped for. I never ever managed it. The idea of it, the smell of him down there – even to this day, that's the smell of sex and I hate it.

He started bringing me in when he was having baths too.

'Shan, come here!' would be the frequent shout from the bathroom. Those three words are enough to set me off even now.

Pass the cloth.

Pass the soap.

Actually, you do it.

Wash me there.

Lower.

Lower, Shan.

That's it, that's it.

Keep going.

And then, the next stage:

In you come.

Just take your clothes off and come in here.

That's it, that's it.

Another layer, another expectation – now it was me in the bath with him, whenever he wanted.

The gulf between me and Alan against Louise was really obvious by this time. Mom and Dad would take her for days out, warning us two not to leave our rooms. Of course, we did, but there was such panic in not knowing when they would be back and having to hide any evidence. He'd started sending me to my bedroom without dinner, but as with everything, there was never a reason for it. They'd order food, things like Chinese takeaway, and I'd wait until they were in bed before sneaking downstairs to get the foil trays out of the bin and lick any sauce off them.

Alan and I were skiving off school a lot and when the truancy officer was sent to our house, we got the beating of our lives with a leather belt. I felt so responsible as I'd encouraged him. There seemed to be no way out of that side of things and all I could do was cling to the moments when Nice Dad reappeared.

The next move was to Shannon when I was eleven. It was a three-bedroom, high-rise apartment near the airport at Drumgeely. That was only for six months and I do wonder why we moved so much – were people copping onto him? Did he move us on to keep off the radar? Maybe neighbours heard us being beaten, maybe teachers finally reported the bruises. It was in Drumgeely that I made my first real friends, Melanie and Nicole. They had a brother called Gary, who Alan was friends with, and a big family that lived just down beside the school we all went to. Even though their dad was an alcoholic, it was still a better home environment than mine. I saw a couple of parents with their kids in a different light and it clicked with me that we didn't have that at all, even without the sexual abuse.

One night, I slept over at Melanie's and had a shocking earache. Their mom heated up some oil and put it in my ear with some cotton wool, gave me a couple of painkillers and sat with me until I felt better. It was a world away from what I had. The girls were always chatting with her and I just didn't have that concept of needing my mother or getting anything back from her. Being able to engage with Melanie and Nicole at school made a big difference to me, I hadn't had that before. I was smoking within a week though, getting into mischief all the time, even though I was quite shy when I wasn't around them for a few days.

We were wild – from smoking at eleven, drinking at twelve, fleecing stuff out of the shops, roaming the streets, other things that I don't even want to admit to. There was a sense of freedom in parts of my life for the very first time. We always had a bag with Polo mints and deodorant to cover the smell of smoking and thought we were so bold.

When we moved to the next house, I got some more friends – Lorraine, Donna and Ava. Lorraine's mother used to cycle up to the school to bring her a special lunch every day and my mouth would drop open. She'd get the shopping on a Thursday and I would be amazed that there was diluting tropical drink, multipacks of Taytos, bars of chocolate – all things geared towards the children and they never needed to ask permission to eat any of it.

Dad never abused me in there, maybe because it was all on one level, but the thing is, even if there is a period in your life where there is no abuse, you don't know that at the time. I was always in a state of fear– just because it hadn't happened yesterday didn't mean it wouldn't happen tomorrow. I would have six months without it but

I didn't know that was coming. When we lived there, I had an almost normal life – he was still violent and horrible, but I did think maybe it would never happen again.

I had hope.

He never spoke of what he had done, never mentioned it, and it had been a while since he'd called me Princess. Combined with the new bits of freedom and my friends, there was more normality. A normality I had never really known.

We moved to the next house, again in Shannon, when I was twelve. Dad didn't work for a year and half in that one, supposedly signed off with depression. Every morning, I'd get up and look out to see if his car was there. If it was, I'd go back to bed as the day would be completely different – maybe I'd get Psycho Dad, maybe not. He had to get a doctor's certificate every week and that landed to me. I'd get the bus to Limerick, go to the doctor, then head to the prison and drop it off for him. As soon as Mom fell pregnant with my next sister, he went back to work but the first bit of time in that house was tinged with him hanging around much more than any of us wanted.

That house was another three-bedroom terraced property – no difference there – very close to my friends. Our house was always spotless and they both wanted 'nice' things. I thought it was all gammy. Old-fashioned and dated, yet they seemed to believe it was the bee's knees. Every house had new stuff in it, but it was that nasty Dutch House furniture with heavy wood and patterned cushions. It was all on the never-never – we didn't own it, it was all about looks. I felt like I was living in a Victorian attic. It was rotten. Everything about my mother was old-fashioned, yet she would still have only been in her early thirties then. She dressed like a granny, she acted like a granny. Skirts past her knee, frizzy short hair, brown lipstick for special occasions and a strip of blusher like it had been painted on – what the feck was going on with her?

'Will you give me a break with that Patsy Cline?' I'd shout at Mom. 'Have you never even *heard* of Madonna?'

She was rushing to be a pensioner. He must have liked her that way because they were still loved up. It was vile, the way they'd sit on the couch holding hands like they were teenagers. I wanted to scream, *he's a fucking pervert, you know!* You think your parents are prehistoric when you're that age and your stomach turns every time they go near each other, but I knew what he was and I knew that she didn't care.

I called that place the House of Doom – it was just abuse, starvation and battering non-stop. I don't remember how it had started up again, but the sexual attacks had once more become part of every single day. And there was no let up from the mind games. I came out of the bathroom one day and went to have a fag out of the window. After that, I walked past him on the stairs.

'Do you smoke?' he shouted.

'No,' I sassed back, 'but if I did, I'd hardly tell ye.'

'I'm asking you a serious question: Shaneda, do you smoke? I can smell it.'

'Yeah, I do – so what?'

'DO NOT smoke in this house.'

For some reason, he meant the opposite. He let me smoke in the house when Mom wasn't there and he let my friends do it too. Everyone smoked back then but there was meant to be at least some pretence that the young ones didn't do it. They all thought he was super cool and such a great dad. He was just messing with my head as always.

Mom got a job in the airport, first of all working early evenings, and Alan would be sent to his room, Louise put to bed and the abuse would start on me, downstairs on the couch. Every single evening, she went to work about 5pm and there he would go. He'd take me with him to collect her at the end of her shift, but first of all we'd go to a viewing area where people went to spot the planes and he'd abuse me there. Nowhere was safe – it didn't matter where we were, it would happen.

Around this time Alan started getting in a lot of trouble with the guards, mostly being caught breaking into houses. He was only about 11. When they came to the door, Dad would reinforce the hatred, shouting that they were never to be allowed in, ask them what they're there for, get their names, tell them nothing. It was weird given that he was a prison officer but it was also the culture of living in Ireland at that time. It worked the opposite for me and I desperately wanted to be a guard when I grew up. The police had a reputation for being lazy, for just sitting around the station and doing nothing to help people, annoying them half the time. I wanted to do good, I wanted to be better than that.

I don't remember the first time he penetrated me, but when I think about that house, that's what it screams to me. Funnily enough, the main thing I recall is the Venetian blinds that went all the way down to the floor. They were always shut when he was in the living room and Mom was out, always angled so no light came in. Any time I think of blinds like that, I get a feeling of pain; I become fearful and there is an agony that goes through me. I can take myself right to the moment. He would often lie on top of me with his penis rubbing against the side of my thigh until he ejaculated as he'd now been doing for years, but the abuse was progressing too.

There was one particular time when he was trying to get nearer and nearer to going inside me.

'Don't! Don't! Don't!' I recall saying, but then I only remember pain. I don't remember the first or second or third time, I just have fractured memories.

He would still be taking me into the bath with him. I think, since he had tried to put his fingers into me in the bath, he knew that couldn't happen, so now the plan was to rape me in there instead. By this stage, despite being older, becoming more aware of things, knowing what sexual abuse was even though I didn't remember where I got that knowledge from, I was still naive. I didn't know that, watching the pornography, he was laying out for me everything he wanted to do completely. When I'd hit eleven or twelve, I knew it wasn't normal and I didn't want it, but I don't know if that was my age or because of the nasty things he was making me do. The pornography was so regular, almost any time Mom was out, and I couldn't help but fear he was going to take the abuse to the next level, to what I had been forced to watch these men and women do for years.

Dad was always one to niggle me – he got a weight bench at that time and wanted me and Alan to try lifting weights.

'Girls can't really do this,' he told me. 'They're weak. Girls give up easily because they're rubbish at everything – sooner you accept that, Shan, the better.'

It fired me up and I always made sure I didn't just lift as much as Alan, I lifted more. It was becoming increasingly obvious to me that girls and women were just seen as second-class citizens. If you had the luck to be born male, you would be privileged and you could treat females like shit. I'm obviously not saying boys don't get sexually abused or beaten, but they still have that maleness which means they are stronger and society sees them that way.

They'll never know the absolute fear that comes simply because you're born a girl.

Dad also started getting back into music. He hadn't bothered in Hicksville, which had meant that I felt I could sing and dance – it wasn't something I associated with him there, it wasn't tainted. Mom spent most of her time in the kitchen when she was at home. You know, looking back, I think the women mostly all did that in those days. Even if they weren't cooking or cleaning – and my dad did a lot of the cooking because of his job – the women would just sit at the kitchen table, maybe reading a magazine, but definitely acting as if that was the place they should be. But I wasn't going to be like that. I'd put Showaddywaddy records on in the living room and twirl about to my heart's content, bawling the songs out at the top of my voice, feeling freedom for at least a little while. In this house, he played Chris de Burgh. I hate 'Lady in Red' with every bone in my body. When Mom's younger brother came to stay for a little while, he opened up other music to me, giving me a Wham! tape and letting me listen to Madonna. For me, that was it. I adored 'Papa Don't Preach', which drove my dad off his head, and I told Mom that I wanted my hair cut like her.

Crying, she took me to the hairdresser, where I asked them to make it short. 'I can't believe you're doing this,' she wept. 'Your beautiful, beautiful hair! What will your dad think?'

But I couldn't give a rat's arse, I also knew he wouldn't be bothered. I was still getting the best of clothes, even if we had no food in the press, and he would just see my hair as fashionable, which was what he wanted people to think of us as a family anyway. The hairdresser took it out of the ponytail and as it fell about my shoulders down my back, my mother started wailing as if someone had died in front of her. I rolled my eyes, delighted that I was getting what I wanted. It was about that time that I became conscious of girls' and boys' bodies, which might sound unbelievable given what I had been through and I thought if I kept skinny and got my hair cut short, maybe people would think I was a boy. Maybe Dad would be less interested.

I could only wish.

CHAPTER 9

Every Day the Same

D ad's temper was destructive in so many ways. Once, I didn't tidy my room properly and he ripped it apart, ruining everything I had, including the dolls from different countries that Grandad had given me when I was small, which he had collected on his travels with the army. They were what I loved the most and I think they were a symbol, to me, of being a little girl. When he destroyed those, he destroyed a part of me. That night, I practically risked my life to go out to the bin and save the one with the orange sari – I couldn't take any more or he would notice. I was devastated as no one else in the whole world had dolls like those and they were the only memory I had of having something that came from Dublin and I didn't want to lose that.

He'd roar if his egg was hard-boiled and he'd wanted an omelette. He'd roar if it was too hard-boiled as well. He'd roar if the door was left open – or closed. If the house wasn't tidy, or he couldn't see us tidying an already spotless room. He would send me to the shops for something and it was timed. If I took too long, I was battered and if I came back too soon, there would be a chance of it too. It was constant and completely unpredictable. I never knew. Yet Louise was saved from all of that.

I was mad for this toy called a Poochie dog, a pink and white creature with fluffy hair that was always being advertised on TV. Every time I heard the song – *well your ears are pink, and your paws are too; just look at all the things they've got for you – it's Poochie!* – I'd beg for one. It was Louise who was given it though, along with a matching duvet cover, whereas Alan and I got these bog-standard covers that would do for boys or girls.

'Why does she get everything?' I asked Mom. 'Why do you never hit her?'

'We learned from our mistakes,' she told me, coldly.

'Really? So why are you still doing it? Have you not learned that much yet?'

If Mom was out shopping at weekends, Dad would make a big show of playing with us. He liked hide and seek the best. Alan and Louise would run around the house, finding hidey-holes, but he kept me with him, pulling us both under the covers on his bed, making me pull at his penis, while my brother and sister were elsewhere, no doubt getting a huge thrill out of the chance they might throw the covers back and find us.

There were still the three dads. The sexually abusive one. The physically destructive one. The normal one with his music and weight benches, teaching us orienteering and taking us camping. It's sociopathic behaviour, if you ask me. He put it all into little boxes and I never knew which Dad I would be getting. For him to do that, I feel he must have known exactly what he was doing. Every moment of every day, he made conscious choices. He was doing things that I had no control over, so I needed to develop a sense of self-worth, which is why I became so competitive, so determined to be better than boys. Maybe developing an eating disorder was part of that small amount of control I had left. Both of my parents had been controlling over food anyway, so by taking the control back, perhaps I felt I was getting one over on them. I was often caught throwing food away, which brought me another battering.

Dad sat opposite me one night as I stared blankly at my plate, refusing to eat.

'You're fucking sitting there until every scrap of that is gone.'

'I don't want it.'

'You don't get to decide. If you're given food, you eat it. Eat it now, eat it in an hour, but fucking eat it!'

I was there three hours until he forced me to eat cold

potatoes, cold vegetables, all the muck I didn't want in my body. It doesn't take much of an expert to work out what was going on there with the two of us battling for control. From the prison kitchen, he'd bring in liver and kidneys, cow's tongues, all that shit, taunting me. He'd shove it in front of my nose before it was cooked, making it clear it was a torment, not that it was just whatever we were having for dinner that night. At twelve, I became vegetarian if I did eat anything at all. I'd try anything to avoid eating. None of it was normal, I know that.

I remember a lot of it, but I have pushed and pushed at my memory – particularly when writing this book and I keep questioning: do I know when he started to rape me?

No. No, I don't.

Memories come in fragments, snippets or scenes that pop into my mind. Being in the kitchen with Alan. Doing the dishes. Friends coming to the door and me telling them I wasn't allowed out. Then, one day, Alan fighting with me, turning me around, kneeing me in the tailbone.

I screamed out with the pain – but this bit is weird.

When Dad came into the kitchen, I didn't want Alan to get battered for doing it.

'What's happening?' Dad asked me.

'I can't tell you in front of Alan.' It was just something I came up with quickly. He sent my brother out of the room and looked at me.

'I'm sore,' I told him.

'What do you mean, you're sore? Where are you sore?'

'It's going right through me,' was the only way I could explain it.

He looked terrified. 'Do you want to go out with those girls? Do you want to call them back?'

Now I was really confused. That was what made me know 100 per cent that he had raped me in that house. When I had said, *it was sore going through me*, he must have panicked and thought I'd roared in pain from him doing that at some point and that I hadn't wanted to talk about it in front of my brother. He needed to distract me, to offer me something, and all he could think of was allowing me to go out with my friends.

As a child, I massively dissociated. I remember these three black spots on the ceiling that I stared at during anything that was going on with the abuse. One time when we went to collect a Chinese takeaway the usual went on, but that time was vicious and I had no memory of it until he brought it up when I was twenty-seven and that's how I know I have blocked so much. It was purely control at that point, to show that he could take me back, mentally, whenever he chose.

When you are abused all the time, it's like making a cup of tea. You think, *sure I'll just let him get on with it and it'll be over.* You get that mentality. I was touching him, he was touching me, he was making me wank him off, he was doing oral sex on me ... I couldn't do that to him though as I kept on gawking. I don't know where it was or what stage but my mind would just lock. A lot of abuse survivors feel guilty because they enjoy the sex – you don't know any better, you're only a child and your body is reacting perfectly normally – but to this day, I don't like sex.

On my thirteenth birthday, I was given a yellow ghetto blaster, waterproof, top-of-the-range – I know now my parents were broke but still trying to keep up appearances – and Dad threw me a party. I didn't want a stupid children's one so he made a big pot of curry with chips, really grown-up, there was loud music, everyone there from my class, about twenty-five people, without any kids' party food in sight – it was like we were being treated as 'real' people.

Wasn't I the lucky one to have a dad like that?

So lucky that he had given me my birthday 'present' earlier that day.

The usual words – 'Shan, come up here!'

But there was something different about that day. It was my birthday, I was a teenager and I'd had enough.

'I don't want to do this any more,' I told him. 'I want it to stop.'

He ignored me, pawing at my clothes, touching me, getting ready to rape me.

'Dad, I don't want this. When will it stop?'

He moved back a little and looked at me.

'I'm teaching you,' he said. 'It'll stop when you enjoy it.'

That would never happen. Even though I knew that was my way out, I couldn't bring myself physically to even pretend I liked it. He wouldn't have stopped anyway, he would have said that it was what I wanted.

Honestly, there were three years in the House of Doom that were all the same. I don't even know what I can say about it, because there was no difference to the days. He was abusing me two or three times every single day. It took me a long time to move on from saying he was 'having sex' with me as I didn't even associate it with the word 'rape' but no more – I know exactly what he was doing. He would say to me, 'I'll go to prison if anyone finds out about this,' and I wanted to have hope that would happen, but every day felt the same and that drains you.

At sixteen, I became really hateful and resentful to him, but it was blossoming from the time I went to high school. You go from being somewhere that is full of little kids to this world of hundreds of people older than you, shouting, making so much noise, talking about all sorts, shoving past you in corridors and there were that many different people there from all walks of life and I saw so much more. That is when and where my personality developed.

Back home, I never had a moment's peace, that's the truth – he was always at me and always ready to do what he wanted to do to me. I couldn't react at home or he would batter me, so I reacted in school. If I was smoking in the toilets and someone said a single word to me, I'd turn around, glare and say, 'Did I give you permission to talk to me?' Being like that was the only freedom I had. I was a walking bitch really. I began to get cheeky with teachers too and pushed the boundaries with the Head of Year. That man, Mr Walsh, had five years of me going on at him. I'd try it with the teachers everyone was terrified of, I was bold beyond belief. I'd get in that zone of just being blinded by anger at everyone. If I was out with friends and an adult started giving out to us, I'd launch into a verbal attack.

'Who the FUCK do you think you are? Fucking talking to us like that! Fuck off, go on!' I'd shout. I took it out on every other adult who ever came into my path.

Harry didn't work for a year and a half before my sister, Eve, was born. He had been signed off work again with depression, but who knows what was going on? I was about thirteen at that point and it was a great idea for him because he could be at home all the time, waiting for me.

'It's your fault,' Mom was keen to tell us. 'You and Alan have made him this way. You've made him that depressed, he can't even do a day's work any more.'

The only thing I knew was with him at home, he could even abuse me at lunchtime. I had thirty minutes every day and he spent every single one of those lunchtimes with his filthy hands all over me if he could. Sometimes I'd actually be in the middle of having my lunch when he would come in and start. The kitchen and the living room were joined by an archway; even if I was in the kitchen, he could see me and decide when to make his move. I was giving out to him by then and I would curse and talk back to him, which would just give him more reason to ground me. It was a routine and on the few times he didn't do it, I would wonder why.

One day, he found my diary and all the stuff I had written in there about how I hoped he'd die, that he was an evil bastard, that I wanted a miserable death for him, but there was nothing about the abuse in it. He kicked me out and told me to come back in an hour once he'd let my mother see it. She gave out to me as well, saying how awful it was that I had said these things about my dad.

'He's not my dad!' I screamed. 'He's your fucking husband!'

That was one of my things at that stage. I called them Harry and Rose whenever I was talking of them and if anyone said 'Dad' to me, I'd say, 'You mean my mother's husband.' If a teacher asked anything about him, I'd say he was 'in' prison rather than working there and that his wife would be visiting him soon.

He would look for any excuse to have me grounded, just to keep me inside for him to get at. I remember being in my room and hanging out the window, talking to my friends, just normal teenage stuff. He would come up behind me and start having sex. They'd all be out there, talking about this and that and everything, stuff you wouldn't want your parents to hear, while he was rutting away at me. I became notorious for slamming the window on people but that was why. The dirty bastard was behind me while I was grounded and only talking to friends. Even if I was at the front door, he would come up behind me and start feeling, so I'd slam the door then too.

He was at me constantly, that's why it all blends in. If we went to Dublin in the car together, he would pull over on the dual carriageway to have a go at me. If we went to collect a Chinese takeaway, he was at me. If we picked Alan up, he was at me. If he took the Ford Granada for a car wash, he'd be at me as soon as the suds started frothing up on the windscreen and windows – I hate car washes to this day, just thinking of him getting me to toss him off.

He always had a hole in the left-hand pocket of his trousers so that I could put my hand in there and wank him while he was driving.

'Here, put your hand in there, Shan,' he would tell me as if it was the most natural thing in the world. And it *was* the most natural thing in *my* world, he'd made sure of that.

He'd make pit stops wherever we went, he was always ready to get his hands over me or get me to touch him. It was two or three times a day every single day, I had no peace of mind.

We used to go camping during the summer, often with a family called the Smiths: two sisters and a brother. Even when we were all in the tent together, he'd get me to go in the sleeping bag with him at night so that he could abuse me. There was a shower block where he abused me. I was terrified all the time, living on my nerves and playing out my constant fear by turning into someone wild. One time when we went camping, there was a group of boys as well as me and one of the Smith girls. We played hide and seek and I was determined the two of us would win. We found them all, then it was our turn. In my head were Dad's constant words of *'men are better than women'* and I made Hollie hide in the middle of a thorn bush with me. She was crying after about an hour. It was getting dark, Dad was screaming for us to come out of hiding, rats were going past us, but I was determined.

'You'd better fucking appear!' he yelled.

'Don't you dare!' I told Hollie. 'We don't give up until they give up.'

I waited until I was ready and that was something I did try to hold on to.

One day, we were cycling and we'd done a good 17km or so already when we got to a hill that seemed almost vertical. It's called Gallows Hill and Dad had been slagging me off the whole way, saying I wouldn't even last to the bottom of it. When we got there, I took off, up Gallows Hill on my bike, almost killing myself in the process, but with a smile on my face when I did it. He'd take Alan and me orienteering, showing us how to follow clues and use a compass, but when my brother was off doing his trail, Dad would have me up against a tree.

Everything was spoiled rotten, everything. It all turned into an opportunity to him, whatever it was.

CHAPTER 10

Accidents

Every family thing we went to, I would straight away think I was inferior to everyone else and get in a state. All I was, in my mind, was *that*. To tell the truth, that continued until I was in my forties, however, my life between thirteen and seventeen in particular was just hellish.

Dad didn't want me leaving the house. There was a double-glazed door put in with locks that he could hear if I tried to get out, he had an alarm system installed that was set when we all went upstairs to bed and if I tried to sneak downstairs, it would go off. He was relentless and calculating. If we went swimming, he'd be at me under the water just as he had been since that twelfth birthday when he taught me to swim and taught me another lesson at the same time – that I wasn't safe even there. If we went to the shops, he would be pawing me, always at me. I never for a moment thought he would be caught as it had been years now; he was too good at it and no one would listen to me anyway. There was no escape. He did it in front of other people, like in the tent, and no one noticed. It was terrifying, it was never-ending. I took on the responsibility of trying to get it done as quickly and quietly as possible but I would never, ever pretend to like it because I knew that was what he wanted. He didn't really talk when he was doing it, just grunted, and he wouldn't have dared call me Princess by this point as I would have just told him to fuck off.

I was fourteen when my sister Eve was born. All I could think of was how embarrassing it was now that everyone would know Harry and Rose still had sex. No one would have dared take the piss out of me though. At school, I was hard. Mom must have only been about thirty-one at that point but she still seemed like an old woman to me, with the way she dressed and the way she acted. I was always trying to draw something out of her, trying to make her more of a person really. 'Why don't you even wear jeans like the other mothers?' I asked her one day, but she just told me to shut up.

I was very aware that I would never become a slave for any man, while she always worshipped my dad – stepping into the role Nanny Daly had performed really. 'Tell him to make his own dinner,' I'd say. 'Why should you have to cook for him? He's perfectly capable.' But it all fell on deaf ears. She was so subservient. He didn't lord it over her, she wanted to do it, she loved it.

My mother was working nights at the airport when she was pregnant with Eve and he had me in the room with him all night on many occasions. I'd have to go to school the next day absolutely exhausted, stinking of him. I was really paranoid about the smell, that sweaty, salty, sex stink that came off him and covered me. It was never just once a night either. I see the longer picture as I'm talking and I can envisage how some things were that I dissociated from. Someone I had sex with when I was an adult told me, 'Being with you was like fucking a rag doll.' It was a horrible thing to say but I know that I didn't move at all once I was a grown woman having sex as that was my response back then too: just lie there.

Dad was always trying to get me to react, to enjoy it, to make moans even like in porn. I would give it a half-hearted, 'aaargh', which was nothing like what he wanted but I would be damned if I was going to perform some sort of consensual, happy sex act for him. I would just stare at a spot on the ceiling and zone out. He didn't care, he was always ready to rape me. I've counted it up and even over those three years in the House of Doom, it must have been well over a thousand times. Later, at the trial, he agreed that there wasn't a day when he didn't abuse me. I might get a week when I went to stay with my aunt and uncle, but even when he collected me with one of my friends, he would get me to sit in the front of the car and be in at the hole in his trousers. As soon as everyone else fell asleep, he'd get me to wank him off just as usual. I'd have a lovely time away and then straight back to that.

All I had, all I ever had, was music and books. I adored 'Personal Jesus' by Depeche Mode and the lyrics spoke to me. I needed someone to hear my prayers, someone to care; I did feel unknown, I did feel alone. I wasn't religious, but the line about reaching out and touching faith meant a lot to me. I wanted to someday get to a point where I could reach out past everything I had been told and everything I had experienced. Another song they did called 'Someone' was such a beautiful track although I could never believe that one day, as the song said, I would almost like all the things I detested about myself. I could almost believe they had written 'Blasphemous Rumours' for me. A sixteen-year-old girl, slashing her wrists, with God having a sick sense of humour and laughing at her when she died? That would fit, that would fit all too well.

I loved The Cranberries too. They toured America with Duran Duran around that time, but when they came back to Ireland, no one cared. Dad worked in the prison with the brother of the lead singer and he gave me a pile of their CDs. There were old songs too – Elkie Brooks singing 'Don't Cry Out Loud' became my motto. I kept everything inside, all the stuff that mattered.

One of my father's things was to make me bend over the banister upstairs to 'check' if anyone was coming up to the next floor – what he really wanted was to have me in that position so that he could rape me from behind. I had never been able to cope with giving him blow jobs but that didn't stop him from trying – sometimes he would rub an ice pop over his penis and make me lick it off. He would constantly force my head down on his penis if I didn't do what he wanted, ejaculating onto my face and laughing about it as if it was the most hilarious thing in the world. I would be spitting and gagging while he shouted at me to, 'Swallow it, swallow it!' There was one occasion when he pinned me to the floor, sort of sat on my chest and held my arms down with his knees. He then wanked himself off until he came all over my face. He loved that.

I was so skinny and sometimes I wonder that he didn't snap me in two as he was a fat bastard. Part of his idea was definitely that, eventually, I would come round and he would have a willing sexual partner. I had it in my head that I just had to get to eighteen. I'd be out of there, I would never have to listen to him (or anyone) ever again.

When the baby was born, they adored her to start with and Dad went back to work. At that time, Mom agreed I needed to go on the Pill but he was the one pushing for it. She'd always told me that if I wanted to talk about sex, I could go to her – the irony of it! I told her that I wanted it, she asked if I was having sex and I told her I might, so best be prepared. She didn't question anything – in fact, she went to the doctor and got it for me. Back then, in a place like the one where we lived, it would be perfectly normal – actually, it wouldn't surprise me if that happened to this day with the old family doctors. I had little connection with my mother so she wasn't doing it out of any protective instinct. My friends would go into town for coffee with their moms, have a good laugh, but none of that happened between us though I was desperate for it to.

I'd wanted another sister but surprisingly didn't have any fear at that point that he would start on her – he wouldn't have the time. I felt as long as I was there, I could protect Eve as he would always be at me. The long game hadn't come into my mind about what would happen when I left at eighteen, when I went off to live my dream life.

He kicked the shit out of me until I was sixteen. I went to the Order of Malta with Alan, which is an organisation like St John Ambulance, where kids learn life skills. I'd go to anything to get me out of the house and Dad liked us going to the Order of Malta, even though he said it was for nerds. We just went for the craic anyway. We learned first aid, got to march in the St Patrick's Day Parade, we visited colleges and were there for events when the Patron came – some prince or other, all of it grand.

We got back late one night and he just flew at us.

'What time do you fucking call this?' he shouted.

'We're on time!' I argued.

'Don't you talk back to me!' He punctuated his words with more slaps and kicks.

I had no idea if we were late or if we were early – probably neither, it was just head-messing stuff as usual. He was obsessive about time anyway: if I was sixty seconds later than I should have been, he decided I was dead. In fact, my watch was always set thirty minutes ahead to try and avoid that, but he made up rules to suit himself anyway. That night, he got the two of us in the corner. His fists and feet were everywhere, raining down on us, non-stop. We were sobbing, breaking our hearts. It wasn't the first time. My hands were always black and blue anyway from trying to protect my face, but that night, he was possessed. He grabbed Alan by the balls and squeezed him as hard as he could, at the same time as he was kicking shit out of me. Then he dragged us into the kitchen and started ripping all the pots and pans from everywhere with scalding water in them (he was always cooking because of working in a kitchen in the prison, so pots of boiling water were usually on the go) and he started screaming about 'fucking bacteria!' and we needed to clean and clean and clean. I was praying for Mom to come home that night but without knowing why. I don't know why I thought she would have saved us as she never would any other time – I hated her.

I'd take a beating for Alan any day. I was older than him and he was even skinnier than me.

There was a time I was sent to the hardware store and forgot my receipt so I was kicked up and down the hall for that. I didn't flinch and he kept on punching the left of my face. He stared at me, furious at my lack of reaction.

'Do you want to get the other side?' I calmly asked, looking him in the eye. 'Looks like you're off your game.'

'Get up to your fucking room!' he screamed at me.

Whenever I went into school like that, bruises and blood even all over my face, it was rare for anyone to notice. If they did, if they asked me what had happened, I'd answer them deadpan and deadened.

'I walked into a wall.'

I was a cheeky bitch but I get angry at it now, those fuckers ignoring that I was always covered in bruises. I had a new friend called Gemma and I would turn up at her house first thing in the morning before school, just wanting to be somewhere else.

Dad became more daring – he never did anything directly in front of Lorraine and Donna though. They were cheeky like me, but Gemma was more polite. When Lorraine and Donna came to the door, he'd say, 'The Degenerates are here.' He didn't think of Gemma in that way but he would be open to her about battering me. I remember crying at the kitchen table when she came in one day and he told Gemma frankly, 'I kicked the shit out of her.' How awful is that? How untouchable did he think he was?

There was nothing I could do to stop him. In bed, I wore

knickers with leggings over them as well as my pyjamas. I'd cut the elastic waistband of my leggings in parts so that I could knot it over me, but it made no difference. There were so many mornings when he was leaving for work at 6am but I'd wake to find his hands crawling up my body. I'd fold myself up in blankets, anything to try and deter him, anything to give me a full night's sleep. It was useless. My period didn't even deter him, he just keep going. Now that I think of it, there must have been blood on his bed – it has to have gone on the sheets – and he wouldn't wash them – so that was all ignored too.

Afterwards, we would sit on the side of the bed and he'd give me a fag while we had a chat about school, friends, family.

'So, how are things with ye?' he would ask. 'Everything OK?'

I'd nod.

Yeh, it's all grand, Dad – apart from you raping me, that is.

Just a nice chat between a girl and her dad. I wonder how my body survived it all. I was so frail, I was always between six and seven stone, practically emaciated with my eating disorder, and it's a miracle he never broke me.

I worked out in that house that he wanted something very specific from me: for him, it wasn't 'just' abuse, it was about making me into a compliant partner really. Mom didn't have much in the way of fancy lingerie, but when I was in the House of Doom, I got to know about the few bits she did have. A white bodysuit, suspenders and stockings were brought out to me one day, with the demand, 'Put these on, Shan.'

'What? You want me to put on Rose's *things*?'

'Go on.'

'No, no, I won't! That's just – that's just weird.'

'Oh, go on – you'll like it.'

He was always convinced I'd like it and I was always certain I wouldn't. I was the one who was right. He wanted me to play the part of his girlfriend; he'd wanted that for a long time, but this? This dressing up in the things my mom wore when they had sex, in the disgusting white bodysuit and stockings? I want to gag even talking about it now. I was still such a skinny thing, but that didn't matter to him – he thought if he dressed me up, I'd be a willing partner, playing the part. It was like he was trying to normalise it all but at the same time acting out his horrific perversions. It reminded me of when I had my appendix out, the nurses had shaved me down below – he loved that and asked me to do it again when it started growing in.

'I like this – do it again, Shan.'

I did it once but then thought, *why in the world should I do things that he wants for this act that I never wanted?* For years and years, I did think he had a split personality – the Good Dad who taught me how to read maps, swim, camp, fish, fix my bicycle and the Evil Dad who abused me, sexually and physically. I don't think that any longer. He is just one man who chose to do those things. He didn't struggle with different parts of himself, he went with what he wanted and what he wanted was to rape his own daughter.

When Mom had Eve, it was clear from the start that she wasn't another golden child like Louise. She was firmly in the same camp as me and Alan. Eve was moved into my bedroom after less than two weeks. I did everything – changing nappies, feeds, getting up in the middle of the night with her.

'Your mother's very old to be having a baby,' Dad explained. 'She can't be expected to do all of this.'

She was thirty-two at that point, hardly an old woman. Even after those first three months, I was expected to do it all. Crying with exhaustion one day, I wept to Mom, 'I can't do it, I can't do this any more. She's up so many times during the night, I'm falling asleep on my feet.'

'That's no good, Shan,' she replied. 'Why don't you have a sit down and a cup of tea for a bit? Get your strength back up again.'

Such kindness, making sure I got sorted so that I could be back to being able to look after her baby! The pair of them were unbelievable.

The presence of Eve even made him think of another twisted addition to his repertoire. I had a friend called Kiara and he would get me to call her.

'Tell her you want to have a bath,' he'd smirk, 'and she needs to come over and look after Eve.'

Kiara was happy enough to do it when I rang. My worry was that Dad would be planning to abuse me in the bath while she was there, but when he didn't come upstairs at all, I let myself relax a bit.

When Kiara left, he edged up to me while I was playing with Eve.

'I like Kiara,' he smirked.

'I do too,' I agreed.

'I particularly like her boobs.' He watched me for a reaction. 'And her fanny. I liked touching those a lot. You should get her back some time.'

I despised it when he told me to ask her round. I felt complicit, but Kiara did come back and every time she left, he would tell me, word for word, what he had done to her. She was a quiet girl and used to tell me her problems, hoping to get me to sort them out, but she didn't tell me about this.

One night, I was upstairs and she was in the living room with him. I was listening out and could hear her getting upset. I think, until that point, I had wondered if Dad was making it up – I hoped he was – but then I could hear Kiara crying.

I flew down the stairs. 'Get out!' I screamed at her. 'Go on, just go!' I couldn't bear being part of it, helping him out, but I also had my reputation to keep up – I was hard, I was a bitch. So, when she started to tell me what Dad had done when we were at a teenage disco one night, I roared at her.

'What are you going to say? Are you after telling people this?'

I went on and on and on at her, frightening the poor girl half to death and she backed down. We met up years later – I apologised and told her that I'd known. We're actually friends now and she's been able to make a good life for herself.

He got away with everything he did for so long. He used to tell me if he'd 'accidentally' let one of my friends see his dick when we were camping, or whether he'd 'accidentally' felt their boobs or arse when we were all swimming. Harry Daly must have felt so much power. He had his own little world and he could do whatever he liked. All I could do was wait for the day when I would be moving on – and pray that I would survive until then.

CHAPTER 11

Marked

There were two newspapers we always got at the weekend, the *News of the World* and the *Sunday World*, for which I would have to cycle to the shop in Limerick. I'd fold them up and put them in the cycle bag, desperate to get home and read all the salacious stuff that was in them. Those papers started me thinking what was right and what was wrong. I'll never forget the story I read in the *News of the World* about a little girl who had been appallingly abused by her father. They said that he even raped her on holiday, in the caravan, and people had seen it rocking while they were inside. That reminded me of the fact that I never, ever got a break from my dad either unless I was physically away from him. They said that she had been abused so much, it had basically hollowed out her insides – which I don't think can be true when I look back on it, but it stayed in my mind. It was seeing it all in those papers which made the link to me, not real life in my own world.

I had been that little girl.

It made me paranoid about my insides. What if my uterus had been damaged too? Had something else been wrecked by him? For years, I thought that anyone I was with would be able to tell because of that story. I was marked forever.

I was sixteen before I had a boyfriend, two months after my birthday. Still wild, I was smoking and drinking, hanging around anywhere if I could get out of the house with Lorraine and Donna, The Degenerates. Dad got a whisper of it and warned me not to go out with him, although he had no idea of who he was. That was the first time I openly defied him, I didn't give a shit what he said.

'If you ever have sex, I'll know,' he told me. 'And I'll kill you.'

Ollie went to a different school but we'd met each other at a dance and then the whole business of trying to get together started. There were no mobile phones in those days, no email or social media, it was just handwritten notes backwards and forwards, people saying that their friend liked you – it's a miracle we managed anything.

It wasn't long before Ollie noticed the bruises that were always covering me.

'What's going on here?' he asked, holding up my hands.

'Nothing, none of your business,' I told him, but when he was holding my head towards him for a kiss, I flinched.

He touched the back of my neck again and I couldn't help but move away – it was covered in bruises, as always.

'Shaneda, how did you get these?' he wanted to know.

'I was just messing about with Alan.' I was embarrassed that my dad was hitting me, but somehow thought a bit of sibling battering was alright.

'And he did this? Christ, I'm not having that! I'm going to have a word with him.'

'No! Please, don't!'

'Why not? He needs to be told.'

I finally admitted it was Dad who had caused all the bruises, but I was mortified that he knew. He was furious.

'This isn't right, Shan, you know that. He can't keep doing this to you.'

'And what am I going to do about it?'

'Something! You have to do something!'

'Trust me,' I told him, 'there's no point. He'd laugh in my face and he wouldn't stop doing it anyway.'

That summer, I got a little job in a shop, which meant I had my own money, mostly to spend on records. I became a lot more sociable and I also had time to think when I was out of the house. Now that Ollie knew about the bruising, he had a lot more questions about my home life and how Dad was towards me. He was a good lad, with a good home on a farm, and it was all of that put together that helped me decide that I would run away – again. So, I packed up everything on my walls, my posters, my cut-out song lyrics from *Smash Hits*, into my bags and went. I left a note for Mom:

You tell your husband, I hope he dies a miserable death. Don't let him come looking for me, I fucking hate him. If you let that bastard come after me, I'll never forgive you.

By that time, Alan was in a REACH Youth Service for children who didn't go to school. It was in the next town and I went there to see if they could help me with getting away from home. There was a priest called Father Sean and Alan brought me into the room to talk with him.

'I want to be put into foster care. I hate my dad, I don't want to go back to my parents,' I told him.

'Well, maybe there's another way,' said Father Sean. 'Would you not go back to the house and talk to your father?'

Talk to him?

'I'll only go back to that house when that bastard's in a coffin!' I exploded.

'Shaneda!' Alan shouted.

'I mean it. I hate that bastard and I'm never going back.'

I left there and then. In between that town and our

town was where Ollie lived. I headed there and walked up to his mother's farm with my bag in my hand. She knew by that time that Dad was knocking me about and I just hoped she'd take me in. A tall, thin woman with a core of steel, she took no nonsense from anyone but also had a huge heart. She'd welcomed me from the start and I just had to pray that she would be open to me turning up unannounced to stay there for a bit while I got my head together. The house was empty as they were collecting Ollie from soccer practice but when Gloria did get there, she was just as supportive as I'd hoped. She went out to have a look about.

'Your dad is driving up and down the road out there,' she told me. 'He won't be able to find the lane with the entrance to us, I don't think, so you're grand here.'

But I wasn't. I knew he'd find me, I knew he wouldn't give up.

That night, I heard the crunch of tyres on the gravel outside and ran from one end of the house to the other. Ollie was trying to calm me down but all I could cry was, 'I'm dead, I'm dead, I'm dead.' Gloria was opening the door as I shook.

'Get her out here now!' Dad screamed at the doorway.

She was calm as anything. 'You want to calm down, Harry.'

'Don't you tell me what to do! Get Shaneda out here now!'

'I'll tell you what I will do, Harry Daly,' she told him, 'I'll stick this shotgun up your hole if you don't shut up. How does that sound?'

He did quieten after that, but I was still terrified.

Gloria came into the living room walking behind him.

'What's wrong with you, pet?' he asked gently, as if he hadn't just been bawling his head off.

Here we go, I thought.

'Don't you be talking shit in my house,' Gloria retaliated. 'You've been warned – is there a part of you wants my gun up your arse? As long as I live, if I ever see another bruise on that girl, I'll be telling the prison service just what sort of man you are. Do you want to go with him, Shaneda?' she asked.

No, I did not.

He stayed there for almost an hour, laying it on thick: 'Your mom misses you. She's heartbroken. She's wondering what she ever did to bring this on. Would you not think of her, Shaneda, would you not come back for her? She's exhausted looking after Eve. Are you not after missing Eve? She'll be missing you, just like your mom is missing you – do you not think you should come home, Shan?' He paused. 'I saw the letter you left your mother. She's very upset. Come on home now.'

I gave up. We were back to him manipulating everything, acting like a good guy – even though Gloria could see right through him. By that stage, it seemed like everything I tried didn't work, he would always find me, he would always get me. Every time there was a spark inside, a little bit of hope that I could escape, Harry would kill it. I had thought that telling the priest that I wanted to go into care would work and then I was sickened when he told me to try and work things out with my father. My hatred towards Harry was becoming so strong that I didn't care how I was going to get away, I'd just keep waiting for those sparks and perhaps one day one of them would work, would carry me to something else.

He was relentless and I could tell he wasn't going to go anywhere. Sighing, I went to pick up my bags.

'Are you sure, Shaneda?' asked Gloria. 'You don't have to, you know.'

'Yeah, I better,' I said, resignedly. 'Thanks, though.'

'Thanks for everything, Gloria,' he said, as if she hadn't threatened to blow him apart. 'I'll drop her off tomorrow for a visit, don't you worry yourself now.'

I thought he would kill me. In the car, I thought, *this is how it ends*. He had seen the letter and he wouldn't let me away with it.

'I can't believe all the stuff you said in that letter about me,' he began. I waited for the punch … and waited and waited. But it didn't come. Just another mindfuck.

The next day, Ollie got his Leaving Cert results, the ones you get before you finish school in Ireland, and Gloria called round the house on the pretence of telling me about them.

I could hear her saying, 'Where's Shaneda?' and my dad replying that I was upstairs.

'I'll get her in a minute,' he told her.

She began yelling, 'Shaneda! Shaneda! Can you come down so I can take a look at you?'

I went down with a big smile on my face. Dad never once hit me again after that, Gloria had managed it. Any time he dropped me off to see Ollie, she would come down to the car and sit with him, keep an eye on him. I saw that woman at a funeral a few years ago and told her how much she had done. She was strong and she inspired me more than anyone to be who I am today. I saw that women didn't have to be doormats.

As soon as I returned home after that episode of running away, the abuse started as bad as ever. It's in my head now about how much dissociation there was, how much I just removed myself, mentally, from what was going on. I could change myself into another person while it was happening, I could cut off a part of my brain. I'd still just stare at the spot on the ceiling and it would become all about that one spot while he did what he wanted to me. He gave out to me still about not moving, not making noises, but I couldn't, just like I could never let him kiss me. That was the only thing I had control over.

Even when he wasn't raping me, he never left me alone. In the kitchen, he'd grab my hips and dry-hump me from behind.

'You enjoying this, Shaneda? Are ye? Are you enjoying it?'

He'd flash me on the landing when I passed and I was a bundle of nerves, wondering if he would do that every single time I saw him. By the time I was sixteen, I was beginning to understand that he actually seemed to think I was his girlfriend rather than daughter. Now that I *was* someone's girlfriend, now that I was with Ollie, an awareness developed that my own father was trying to build that with me.

Although I was a girlfriend, there was one part of my relationship with Ollie that I wasn't ready for. One night, we all went drinking and ended up in a house God knows where. I was determined I was going to have sex with him. Completely langered, I was drunk off my face, and I was going to get this out of the way. Ollie was off to college by then and one of his friends was always on at me: 'Have you given him his going away present?' or 'You'll have to give him a present for coming back home.' I'd had enough of giving those sorts of presents to Dad on his birthday and Christmas, but I felt that now was a time when I had to do this disgusting thing on my terms. Of course, they weren't my terms really given that I was feeling pressured by what was expected of me, but I persuaded myself otherwise.

Gloria had even asked if we were having sex and when I told her we weren't, she said that he must really like me. He was a nice lad, but even nice lads only wait for so long.

I took him by the hand and led him up to a bedroom in the house we were all in. Lying on a bed covered in coats, with music and noise blaring from downstairs, I decided this was it.

I couldn't do it.

Just as Ollie was about to do the deed, I shouted out, 'No! I don't want this!'

He was absolutely fine. He took his hands off me and was completely reassuring and didn't even ask anything. He never pressured me for all the time we were together and we never did have sex for the nine months of being a couple. Eventually, I ended it just as I end everything. We'd had a stupid argument and his friend said to me, 'Ollie thinks you should have a break.'

'Does he now? Well, tell him that he can have a breaking forever – will that suit him?'

There was a plan to meet up after a bit, for a reconciliation I guess, and I went into town with a friend to meet him. While she popped into a shop, I had other plans.

'I just need to make a call,' I told her, heading to the phone box. 'Hi Mark,' I said to a good friend of Ollie, 'I'm meant to be meeting your man later – could you give him a message from me?'

'Sure, Shaneda, sure.'

'Could you tell him to GO FUCK HIMSELF?' I yelled, then slammed the phone down.

Broken-hearted, even though I'd brought it all on

myself, I lay on my bed listening to depressing songs – 'All Out of Love' on a loop, stuff I wouldn't give you the time of day for now. So, I cut off my nose to spite my face and I would do that for the rest of my days. I couldn't help myself. With men, I would always get there first before they did. I made sure I destroyed them before they could destroy me. By sixteen, to the outside world there were no soft parts to me, I was seen as a hard bitch and that was fine. I would take no prisoners, go for the jugular, I didn't give a shit – and that meant no one would ever guess what I was going through at home.

CHAPTER 12

The Beast Inside Me

———

I spent all my money on music. When I tried to run away again when I was sixteen, I told Donna and Lorraine that my dad had sexually abused me until I was ten.

'Jesus, that's awful, Shan,' they said, then we just moved on. 'What records did you buy with your wages?'

Why I thought that age range I'd told them about was OK, I don't know, but I didn't want them to know it was still happening. I did tell them I'd had enough, though.

'I'm fucking going. I'm leaving and I'm never going back.'

'Good on ye,' said Lorraine.

'Fair play,' agreed Donna.

We all waited in a back road, as I decided to hitch to the next village where Ollie lived. I wanted my friends to see what car I got into in case I was murdered. After a while I gave up and just went home. The abuse was never brought up between us again and neither were any of my many failed attempts to leave.

The girls were knocking on the door for me, New Year's Eve, and Dad went psycho. He never usually roared in front of them, but finally, he said I could go out for an hour. So, I got a jumper from Donna and went to Dublin. I was heading to my Auntie Janey. Her house was over a dodgy field and I couldn't get there as it was so dark, which meant I had to go to Auntie Elaine on the other side of the field.

'Hi – I came to visit, how are you?'

'We're grand, thanks – were you just passing? In the night? In the dark?'

'Yeah, I was so,' I told her.

Then she copped I didn't have a bag.

Elaine phoned my mom, her sister, who said she wanted to talk to me. Mom was upset, to be fair. My uncle put me on the bus the next day and said to the bus driver, 'Don't let her off until she gets to Limerick.' He did as he was told and I hitched to Shannon with a neighbour. Dad was at the first bus stop, waiting for me. I went straight to Lorraine's house, where her mom fed me, and I waited for two hours before giving up and going home. Dad was roaring when I got in, laying down the law, but for some reason, Mom gave me a vodka and coke.

Little things were happening: I was determined I was

going to win, I was going to break him. He was not going to get the better of me. It was a constant battle. I was becoming stronger even if my anger did get the better of me on many an occasion.

Bryan Adams' '(Everything I Do) I Do It For You' was in the charts for all the year I was sixteen, but my role model was Wendy James out of Transvision Vamp. She was this tiny little blonde thing, but she had such an attitude and I adored that. I had a lip gloss called *Pink Illusions*, which was just the same as the one she wore, and I thought I was it with that on. All my friends were into Kylie and Bros, but it was Wendy James for me – and Metallica. I had been introduced to them when someone put their headphones on my ears and when I watched them at the Freddie Mercury Tribute Concert, I saw the lead singer with his swinging hair and undercut and I just loved them.

Music gave me happiness and I disappeared into it whenever I could. I never wanted to be in a band myself though – strange as though it might seem, I still wanted to be a police officer, a guard. At a careers event in school, there was a woman there who was really nice and it seemed something that would fit well with my height (you had to be tall), so why not? Dad had always told us not to trust the garda, not to even give them our names, and it would have been a great kick in the teeth to him. I had to leave school at 17 though – I was actually kicked out as I had no legal guardians having left home and that was a legal requirement – and so that put an end to that. The only certainty was despite looking after Eve all the time, I definitely didn't want kids. They were annoying, I was completely disinterested in them and I never ever saw myself as a mother when I looked into the future.

Once, when I was about sixteen, I was in the kitchen and Dad was kicking the shit out of me – there was never a reason. I was near the washing machine while he kicked and kicked me. He had steel-capped boots on from work and that was the only time ever that my mother said, 'Leave her alone!' He looked at her and she said, 'I mean it, I'll leave.'

A few minutes later, she had her jacket on.

'Where do you think you're going?' he asked her.

'Work,' she told him.

What a bitch, she was never going to leave because of me, I thought.

I guess he must have known the extent to which he could hit me, how far he had pushed it, or I would have been beaten to death or had something broken. He did have an anger on him, a rage, and he never walked away until that was out of him, but there had to be something that acted as a barrier. If he had broken something on my body, the whole house of cards would have toppled as there would have been people from outside the family having to come in.

On the day of Eve's christening, his sister was there

while he kicked hell out of me – she's dead now. He was really going for me, not a care in the world that we had a houseful, when Debra shouted at him, 'Don't hit her on the head, Harry!'

At last someone was sticking up for me.

'Never hit them on the head. You can cause damage if you hit them there, go for anywhere else,' she explained. She must have done that to her kids too – maybe it ran in the family? But if Dad was able to stop himself from hitting Louise, he obviously had some control.

I was with Ollie at the time and I still hadn't had sex with him. I didn't plan to because I was terrified that he would know something was wrong with me. Fellas were always saying to girls that they knew that they could tell if they were virgins but I thought they would also know that there was something in me that was wrong because of the abuse. I genuinely believed that something inside me had changed because of what Dad had done to me.

Back then, I was still at school and I was doing well, but no one ever picked up on anything while I was there. It wasn't as if I didn't give them signs. I had to do a project and so I did mine on child abuse. I did lots of research on it, studied sexual, physical and emotional abuse. It had all been started off by that little girl I had read about in the *News of the World* and it was much easier to access information in newspapers than anywhere else. Everyone else was doing theirs on the President of Ireland, but not me.

It wasn't the first time I looked into this. When I was in the third year, everyone was given the same first sentence and told to write an essay:

Nobody thought it could be done …

They all wrote about flying to the moon and other nonsense like that. My essay began: *Nobody thought it could be done by such a man.* It was all about sexual abuse too, but no one asked any questions. It was a huge red flag and completely ignored – I got top marks and that was it. I wasn't one bit surprised, but I did feel empowered and bold that I had done it in the first place – and done it well.

Exhausted the whole time, I started mitching (bunking off) school a lot. It was a nightmare, but I was clever anyway so I could catch up. I had a friend called Maria who was fed up with living at home too, so we were talking about renting a room off this fella Robin in the next road. We were taking bits and pieces out of our parents' houses and hiding them in our rooms – pots and dishes, that sort of thing.

It all came to a head one night when Dad owed me money for babysitting but told me I couldn't have it. When I went out, I left one of my notes to Mom:

Tell your husband that I've been to the guards and they said I could leave home once I had a job.

It was all lies – I hadn't been to the guards at all, but it was true that I had a little job in a canteen washing dishes. I'd been there at weekends, but they had asked if I wanted more shifts. I would leave for school and go there instead. That night, I took £20 out of his jacket, the money he owed me, and left. All of the pots and pans, etc. had been taken out that day, they were all at Robin's flat waiting for us. It was an absolute dive. I was an expert at household stuff as I'd watched Mom do it for years, so Maria and I wallpapered one wall in our room to make it girly, different from all the boy stuff in the rest of the house, but it didn't hide the fact that it was a truly disgusting place. Mom was going over to Lorraine's house every day, wailing and weeping, asking where I was, with no idea that I was only a couple of streets away. Rose could make anyone feel guilty and Lorraine had to stick to her guns, keeping to her word that she wouldn't tell her. On the third day, my sister Louise came to tell me Rose knew where I was.

'Tell her to go fuck herself,' I said, adamant I wanted nothing to do with her. I closed the door on her, but within about half an hour, one of the lads living with us shouted on me that Rose was there. I opened the door, looked at her and slammed it in her face. That night, a letter was handed to me from my father – *please come over and talk to us, we can't believe this has happened*, all that sort of thing. So, I went to see them, telling Lorraine that if I wasn't back in an hour, she should ring the guards.

Dad was in the living room, making a show of himself. It was the first time I had ever seen him crying.

'I don't know how it's come to this, Shanny,' he moaned. 'Come back, will you?'

'You only want a childminder,' I told him.

No way was I going back.

As I've said, Robin's flat was a horrible place but Maria and I cleaned up and made the two fellas living there their dinners to help out. Nothing had been decorated in about twenty years. We scrubbed the whole flat and did as much as we could to make up for the cheap rent. The canteen job ended as it was only temporary and eventually I had to sell my stereo and other things to pay the £10-a-week that Robin asked for. Eventually, Rose got me and Maria and Lorraine some evening shifts cleaning and that helped a bit.

My parents asked me to move back in for Christmas and I did. I missed my siblings so much but never really thought about them being abused – I know that sounds selfish, but I honestly thought I'd kept it to me by doing pretty much everything Dad wanted over the years. I did worry about them being in such a toxic atmosphere though, but that was more general. The guilt again. Dad told me that I could do what I wanted, there would be no rules, I could be me. I'd been kicked out of school as I had no legal guardian once I moved out, which put paid to my dream of joining the police. On Christmas Eve, I went to someone else's house for a party and the same on Christmas Day itself. It was hardly idyllic.

On Christmas morning, I got up as Dad was going off to work. He pinned me to the kitchen counter and was grinding against me. Afterwards, I struggled back to bed with a hangover from hell. When I woke up, he had his hands under the blanket, in my knickers.

'Get the fuck away from me!' I roared.

He did leave, with a smirk on his face and this time I decided that I was leaving for real. So, I did walk out – a lovely Daly Christmas, as always.

It was almost 1993 and I was three months away from turning eighteen. In my mind was the idea that I'd never have to listen to anyone ever again once I hit that point. For about two months I was at Robin's flat, on and off. I did go back to see Mom every so often, although never when Dad was there. I went because I had no money and it was somewhere I could help myself to food. As always, she was tight with it though – one time refusing me a slice of bread, which meant that I had to get in quickly and make myself something before she could stop me.

I became friends with a girl called Carly who was renting a room two doors down from the flat. She was a couple of years older than me and was one of the first people I told about Harry.

I was really drunk in a nightclub when everything built up inside me and spilled out. The disco part of the pub had a table, where I was sitting with her. There was broken glass and I ended up slitting my wrist, then telling Carly so much of what was in my head. I was talking directly into her ear as it was so noisy: we were cheek to cheek, talking in each other's ears.

Back then, I didn't know when to stop drinking, it always got very messy and I'd end up an emotional wreck. There were people all around us, loud music, everyone else talking.

'What's wrong?' she asked as she bandaged up my wrist with pub napkins. 'Tell me, Shaneda – what is it?'

'It sounds mad, but my dad was abusing me and I only got away two months ago,' I finally admitted.

She hugged me so tightly.

'It'll be OK, Shan, you'll be OK – but it's not right.' She kept me in her arms but there was very little else I wanted to say.

Sometimes it's easier to tell a stranger than a friend. Maybe that was what was going on there. So, I told Carly everything, how long, what he had done. I said to her that he had been sexually abusing me all my life, I hated him, I hated myself, I had to get away. I didn't feel loved or wanted. I was so emotional all the time. It had been building, for sure. Carly was so kind and caring. I was still drinking and getting more upset as I told her – it was always the way with me. Carly had her arm around me, consoling me, holding my hands. She'd put a scarf over my wrist and was telling me everything would be fine.

'We'll talk tomorrow when you're sober, you're not on your own now.'

It felt like a watershed in a way. Carly took me under her wing. She started to call for me and bring me down to her house, where it was calm, not like the crazy place where I lived, which was always party central. Slitting my wrist that night had been a spur-of-the-moment action, but then it became a thing with me: any time there was a broken plate or glass, I would hurt myself. For the next couple of months, I cut myself whenever I could – it wasn't to kill myself, it was to feel pain.

Around the time that I told Carly about the abuse, I also told her that I hadn't had a period since I moved out of home.

'It'll be stress – no wonder,' she soothed.

'I don't know, Carly – I just have this feeling. Not physically, but in my mind.'

Carly knew what was what. 'I'll get you a pregnancy test,' she told me.

'Will you? I haven't a clue about anything, I haven't a clue about any of this.'

'It'll be grand,' she promised. 'You'll see.'

Some time later, she brought back a package and told me to pee into a cup. Then she did whatever was needed for the test. I couldn't bring myself to look at the little plastic tray.

Carly was quiet for what seemed like an age and then,

with a sigh, she placed her hand on mine and said, 'It's positive, Shaneda. You're having a baby.'

I was in a panic. What the fuck was I going to say to people? This child was my father's, for sure. I hadn't been with anyone else. He'd always told me to wash inside so that there was no sperm left but it clearly hadn't worked – little wonder given how often he abused me. Almost instantly, I believed there was a monster growing in my belly with fifty heads and fifty arms and fifty legs. We'd all heard stories about incest and what the babies were like – I was one of those stories now. The last time he had raped me was when I had left in the October, and now it was the end of January 1993 – I was probably about three months gone.

Everyone was so close amongst our friends and in our community, I wouldn't be able to hide it. I needed a story and so I did something in my panic that was really awful.

'It's Jake's,' I told Lorraine, naming a friend of her boyfriend. 'It's his baby.'

'Jesus, Shan, that's a shocker! How the fuck did it happen?'

I had to think on my feet. 'We were both drunk – I don't think he'll even remember, to tell you the truth.'

It was as simple as that. None of us slept around so there was no way she would have believed it was anyone out of our circle and we were both so naive, it all seemed perfectly plausible. Of course, I felt guilty, but I knew Jake, he was a lovely lad and he would just be bewildered. It's horrific to think back to what I did, and how I did it so instantly, but I have told the truth about all of my story and don't ever want to sugar-coat times when I was less than perfect – this was one of those times.

CHAPTER 13

'I know a woman ...'

I had no idea what to do. You have to remember what Ireland was like back then. Sex education was done by the nuns and they would never have mentioned abortion. I vividly recall the one who taught me at school. She paused the video at the very moment the baby was coming out of the woman and it showed everything. *Everything*. When the nun started the film up again, in slow motion, we saw this woman being ripped open and blood practically hitting the screen. It was horrific, my stomach turned and I was completely traumatised.

'This, THIS is what you will go through if you commit sin,' she'd told us. 'THIS is the reality of sex before marriage. If you go on the Pill, you will go to HELL. Unmarried mothers are FLAUNTING SIN in the face of God. What will you choose? WHAT WILL YOU CHOOSE?'

Jesus, there was no way I would have been ready for that even if it hadn't been Harry's child. My head was all over the place – I'd be giving birth to his child and his grandchild. Would I also be giving birth to my own brother or sister? I had no idea. Desperately trying to bring on a miscarriage, I drank as much as I could. There were hot baths too. I only knew one girl who had gone to England for an abortion – the cousin of a friend – and she'd had a nervous breakdown afterwards. I didn't think she had done anything wrong; to me, it was her decision, I just felt bad for her that she was suffering. We all heard that you 'went on the boat' but it became a phrase that encompassed everything to do with abortion, even if you didn't actually go on a boat at all. It was symbolic of every part of the backward thinking of Ireland – the lack of respect for women's rights, the belief that the Church got to decide everything. There was no education on what to do if you fell pregnant and certainly none on what to do if you didn't want to keep the baby. Maybe the Catholic Church thought they were helping or protecting you by saying nothing, but that wasn't the case at all, it just bred ignorance. There were stickers for one helpline for 'unwanted' pregnancies, but it just got you in the system for the Mother and Baby Homes.

Almost certainly, every generation believes they are the generation that won't listen to that shit any more but it gets under your skin. Seeing that woman on the video, seeing her rip, was not something I could ever go through. Since the day I watched it, I was after asking every woman I knew who had a baby, 'Did you get stitches? Did you rip?' I was obsessed. Now it was a reality and there was no way I could do it. We had always been told that abortion was killing your baby but what option did I have?

I had no symptoms at all – I wasn't sick or nauseous, I hadn't put on weight, I wasn't tired. If it hadn't been for the test, I wouldn't have known, I would have just thought Carly was right about stress making me miss a few periods. I didn't go to a doctor – what would be the point? That would only put me in the system. I wouldn't be able to access an abortion legally, which meant if I did see a GP, they would want to know why I was no longer pregnant if I did get rid of it. Carly was there for me and no one ever challenged me on my lie of sleeping with Jake. He was sure we hadn't had sex, but I just kept saying he was drunk and didn't remember.

I was so naive about it all. I thought that a baby was inside you as a blob of cells that came together at the end to be a baby. Carly was always telling me I would be OK, saying she would help, whatever I decided. She said if I had the baby I'd be fine, I'd get support, I'd get a council house, but all I could think was that I was having an alien. I couldn't do it. To me, it was disgusting, I was repelled. I wanted it gone from my body. I never ever explicitly told Carly it was Harry's child but she must have guessed. I was drinking all the time, trying to block everything out as well as get rid of the baby. I'd heard stories of girls who had drunk spirits then thrown themselves down the stairs – I wouldn't do the stairs thing, but I kept trying the drink.

Honest to God, we were like hillbillies: no education, no awareness of what to do really. Carly was strong and wise though – she took no shit from anyone and she'd be my saviour through this mess. I spent a lot of time sitting on her bed talking because my other friends were even more naive than me and they'd be no help. I was always willing to talk to people, but they were stand-offish so they knew even less, which meant that Carly was the only one who knew the extent of the abuse I'd been through.

It was maybe six weeks after the test that I knew I wanted an abortion. There was a realisation that the drinking wasn't working and I wanted it gone. I felt sick at the thought of it, I wanted it out of me. It would come out looking like Harry, I knew it. My head never stopped spinning.

'I know a woman ...' Carly told me one day.

Words that so many women have said to so many other women over the years. When she said it, I knew this was my way out. If I didn't do it, my life would be over. It was the only way I could give myself a chance.

'Where?' I asked.

'Limerick.'

'Will you sort it all, Carly?' I begged.

'Yeah, sure I will.'

Do you know, even writing about this almost thirty years later, there's a part of me wonders if I can still get in trouble. When I'm thinking of what I did, what I sought out, the Church and the nuns are in my head. I'm not religious. I believe that you should be a good person as far as you can, walk your own path and make the right choices. But I also know that I was brought up in a country where I would be regarded by some people as worse for ending a three-month pregnancy than Harry Daly for thousands of acts of abuse. I'm wary of talking of this, I really am, but it has to be said.

I got the bus into Limerick with Carly – I didn't know the address and just followed her lead on everything. We were absolutely langers, smoking joints, off our faces – trying our hardest to be oblivious to it all, I guess. Carly knew where the house – the woman – was and must have been in contact with her as it was all organised.

We walked to a normal place on a residential street. The door opened and an ordinary woman in her mid-forties welcomed us in. The house was clean and tidy, completely average. She brought me into what looked like a spare room, there were no signs that people slept there, and told me to lie down on a bed.

'Now, Shaneda,' she began – I hadn't even thought to

give a fake name – 'I'm just going to give you an internal examination, is that OK?'

She was really nice and friendly.

'I don't want to know – just do it,' I said.

Meanwhile Carly waited in the living room downstairs.

'I'll try my best, but I can't guarantee this will work.'

She seemed concerned and when I look back on it now, I think she might have been a nurse. You must have to be trained to do those exams and work out how old the baby is from feeling about. She had her hand inside me then stopped to collect everything she needed. It was as if she got a funnel with a tube going into my private parts and then liquid was being put into that. I was so drunk, I was oblivious. Once she finished putting the stuff inside me, she handed me some tablets – I was to take them at two different times to try and finish the process.

'Go home, stay in bed and see if anything happens.'

I went back and kept drinking, blocking it out. Carly was staying there anyway and normal life was going on in all the other rooms, noise and laughter seeping through to me. It was the next morning, as I was sobering up, that the cramps began. It was like period pain but a million times worse than anything I had ever experienced. I started drinking again, throwing back painkillers, throwing back more drink, then I went into the bathroom and everything gushed out of me into the toilet. There was more blood than I'd ever seen in my life but I had been sort of prepared for that; I did think that an abortion would have to contain loads of blood, I wasn't that daft. There was one huge cramping – a contraction, I guess – that almost ripped me in two, then I felt something else come out of me. A huge plop is the only way I can describe it.

I never looked; I flushed it away and never looked back.

Afterwards, the pains and blood for a few days made it hard to even get out of bed, but I held on to the fact that the relief was huge.

The monster had gone.

It was sometime in the next few days that Mom asked me to go over to her house as she'd heard I was sick. I went over to see her and when I was sitting on the couch, I saw a full bottle of Smirnoff on the wooden display unit – there from Christmas, I guess. I was loving drinking then and my eyes were drawn to it like a jewel. The more I could drink, the more I could forget – and I'd forget a lot with a full bottle of vodka. So, I got up and put it down the back of my jeans, then left. I was almost at my house when Alan arrived behind me, saying, 'Give me the drink!'

'What are you on about?'

'The vodka, I've to take the vodka back!'

'I've no idea what you're talking about!' I screamed.

I'd been drinking all day anyway. It went into a fight, he was swinging me around and I shouted at him, 'That's it! I'm going to the cop shop and pressing charges against you for battering me!'

'Come on so, I'll go with you!' he taunted.

Off we walked together, to the cop shop, and I was cold as hell when I went in.

'Hello there, I'd like to press charges against my brother please, for assaulting me.'

The guard was just staring at me.

'She's got the vodka! She's got the vodka!' Alan was bellowing.

I stared at him. 'I have no vodka,' I announced. 'But I do want him charged. And … my father for sexually abusing and RAPING me for years.'

With that, Alan boxed me in the face and tried to throw me over the counter. The guard came out from behind and grabbed him, while my brother shouted, swearing at him to get away. He got arrested for that and dragged into the back. The guard came over to me, where I was sitting down, watching it all.

'Are you OK?' he asked.

'I'm fine – and I most certainly do not drink,' I lied, swaying about and completely off my face.

The guard said nothing about my allegation against Harry, not a word. I sat there for a while, then walked out. Lorraine found me outside the school, unconscious and oblivious, on the ground, full of drink. They tried to wake me up as Alan and Rose walked towards us all. My brother had been let out but hadn't learned a lesson as he tried to get at me again – Rose stopped him, picked me up and took me back to my flat, not her house. She'd been told in the cop shop what I'd said about Harry, even though they'd let it slide. I heard a few days later from Rose that Alan had got a knife when he got home and tried to stab Harry, but Rose stopped him. Like everything else, it was never mentioned, never looked into, just brushed under the carpet like so many other Daly family secrets.

Around 6am the next day, there was a knock on the door: Harry. He came in while I was lying over two chairs – the mother of all hangovers – and asked me to come over to the house: 'Your mom wants to talk to you.'

'I don't want to come, I want my dad.'

'Ah, Shan, I'm here now,' he coaxed.

'Not you! I don't want you.'

Maybe some things do come out in drink, maybe I was honestly saying how much I wanted a father, a real father, not this sorry excuse for one. I ran upstairs and jammed the wooden length of a broom under the door handle so he couldn't get at me. I heard him leaving, then Rose arrived later. She was so angry.

'You get dressed now – get the fuck over and prove what you said was true!'

By then, I was vomiting, the vodka coming up like phlegm, forcing me to taste every bit of it again. I couldn't really argue with her.

'You ring the prison,' she told me when we got in. 'Ask for your dad and tell him you're sorry.'

149

I can't even remember what I said to begin with, but I had no intention of apologising to that beast. I would ask him though – I would finally ask him: 'Why? Why did you do that to me?'

'You know why. You were always my favourite.' He wouldn't stop saying it. 'You were my princess, you were everything to me.'

Rose was on another phone, listening to it all.

'How do I know you didn't do anything to my sisters?'

He gave a dry laugh. 'I've told you – because you were my favourite. I've always loved you, it was always you.'

After throwing the handle of the phone I was holding at Rose's head, I walked out, one tear rolling down my face. I went back to my house, which was crazy as usual, to sit numbly on the couch before I started bawling. I wasn't thinking that people would know and it would be awful, I just wanted him to stop and to get him out of the house forever. I never thought for a second Rose would stay with him once she knew.

I got a message to say she needed me and to get over there immediately. She was hysterical.

'He left, he left, he packed his stuff, he's gone!' she wailed. 'My Harry's gone!'

She was roaring so badly, I had to go get one of her friends. I also went to the shop and got two bottles of wine and lay on the sofa knocking back the wine while she got on with it. When she finally went to bed, I got a knife and put it under the cushion on the sofa, terrified Harry would come for me. He wouldn't get to touch me if he did. He'd kill me, no way would he let me get away with this. There was no comfort from Rose. He was gone, she was devastated, she couldn't cope – that was the script.

CHAPTER 14

Romeo and Juliet

———

The next day, I was taken to see a social worker. All I wanted was a letter – I'd been trying to get money from the social welfare for ages to give me the means to live away from my parents, but I had to get a letter from a guard, a priest or a social worker who knew the situation at home. Basically, I had to prove to them that my parents were psychos. Rose had been down to the local centre and made the appointment. She was all over the place, helping me sometimes, calling me a bitch at others. When we went in, I was dissociating from everything. I had my resting bitch face on, looking like nothing bothered me.

I was the best actress in the world.

I answered with as few words as I could get away with.

'When did it start?'

'I was small.'

'What age?'

'Couldn't talk, that sort of age.'

I told the woman some things eventually and looked up to see her weeping.

'Why are you crying?'

'Do you not think this is absolutely devastating?'

Her headband flopped forward onto her forehead and I started laughing, focusing on that in the way people laugh when they've been told something awful, trying not to concentrate on the reality.

'Oh, just give me the letter for social welfare and sort yourself out!'

Mom took me to the Rape Crisis Centre the next day. Why was that? Because she knew I hadn't been lying. Harry had stood there before her and said to her, 'Everything Shan says is the truth. You need to bring her to Rape Crisis.' What a great dad. He had said all of that once he had 'left'. I'd soon find out they were in touch all the time and his leaving had been all for show anyway.

Rape Crisis was in a lovely Georgian building with cosy, puffy couches and there was no pressure on me at all. Your woman there, Ingrid, was fantastic. We sat down, I was given a cup of tea and was my usual bitch: 'I don't want to talk about it.'

'That's fine, you don't have to. Just sit here and have a cup of tea.'

The woman went in to see Rose who was in a different

room and who had ranted on for two and a half hours, while I sat there twiddling my thumbs, listening to *The Gerry Ryan Show* on the radio. Gerry had been the first one to give a voice to rape victims. On one programme he had asked a woman if she wanted to give her name and that was such a big statement in Ireland. That one action allowed Victim Impact Statements to come through in Ireland – these allow you to say, in your own words, how a crime has affected, or continues to affect you. I felt like it was a symbol to hear him on the radio that day. As I sat there, I smiled to myself, thinking Rose had even managed to make this all about her as usual. Years later, I found out from the woman who spoke to her – Ingrid – that there hadn't been a single tear for me, she cried only for Harry. It was such a relief for someone to acknowledge what I already knew.

The day at Rape Crisis was definitely about her, but I felt that it might be somewhere I'd go back to. The trip to the social had been a bit of a success as I got some money, which meant that I didn't have to go to Rose's as much, but she couldn't cope and by God, did everyone hear about it. Her man had left, her daughter was saying all sorts and she was left alone without Harry, which must be the worst thing that had ever happened in the history of the world.

I had never really thought she would be there for me, but I needed someone. I hadn't seen my Aunt Imelda since I was fifteen, but I often thought about her. She was the best of the bunch: cool, trendy, with a nose piercing and a love of Metallica. It came to me that she would be a safe port for this storm – at least, I hoped so. I got in touch with one of my cousins, Michael, to see if he could ask his mother if I could visit her in Dublin.

When I got there, all I could say was, 'I need to tell you some things.'

'You talk as much as you like,' she said.

But I couldn't do so to her face: 'Can we go to the bathroom?' I asked.

Imelda never flinched, never asked why. She just nodded and followed me. I didn't turn on the light – I didn't want her to see my face when I spoke those words. She sat on the edge of the bath and it all poured out of me in the dark. What Harry had done for years, what he had admitted to doing. From that day Imelda has loved, supported, believed me, never doubted me and been like the mother I always wanted.

'You can stay with me any time,' she told me. I did – for nine months.

Meanwhile Rose was definitely still seeing Harry. She had money, she was staying away overnight, suddenly she had new lingerie. When I realised she was actually having sex with him, something ripped inside of me.

'After all you know!' I roared. 'After all you fucking know, Rose!' Howling with pain, I smashed every ornament in her house. I ripped both my wrists with one of the shattered pieces, shouting that she was a whore to anyone who would listen. As she went out, she slammed the door behind her, not willing to face me – like so many times before.

I was still there when she came back the next day.

'You're back, are you? You whore!'

At this, she lunged at me, pinning me against the wall. 'NEVER call me that again!' she screamed into my face.

'How could you have sex with him, you whore? How could you do it, Rose, you whore?' I wanted the word to wound her.

'Do you not understand? I miss him, I love him,' she said, suddenly crumbling. Her sickly-sweet voice disgusted me, the way she melted when she spoke of him.

I went upstairs, got my bag and went straight to Imelda. Having my life filled with him, never leaving me alone, then for her to just betray me – again – was unforgiveable.

'She's a stupid bitch, an eejit,' said Imelda. 'Her need for him is bigger than anything else and she'll never learn.'

No one ever came to check on me. I was only seventeen and no one ever came to that door to see if I was OK. The anger is there now. It's only when I look back on it, I can see how wrong that was – back then, I was glad I didn't have to give the whole story. I only ever said I had been abused at that point, I never gave a detailed list of what he had done to me and no one asked. Music got me through. I listened to The Cranberries on a loop – their words made so much sense to me. Still obsessed with Depeche Mode, I played them constantly. All music that had no link to my dad, it was just mine and it got me through.

He was only gone from January to Christmas Eve, 1993 – Rose started going to see him at the prisoners' mess and staying over every Saturday. I wouldn't even look at her when I went back to collect my money, I spent as much time as I could with Imelda. As soon as I hit the road to my aunt, Rose would have Harry in there. At some stage when I was still in Dublin, someone put a note through the door saying, *Get Dirty Harry Out*. Rose was shocked that anyone could be so cruel to her lovely husband.

'People are terrible,' she whinged. 'That's the truth. They just want to be hurtful.'

She had this ability to section things off – he was her husband and I had ruined her relationship with him. I used to want to hit her on the head to see if she had any brains in there. She would tell me things as if I wasn't the person her husband had abused, just nattering on about how terrible her life was. I think if she'd supported me, I would 100 per cent have forgiven her. My life would have been so different, had my mother been there for me. Already I had been through a lifetime of pain but Harry was out of the house, making a pretence of getting therapy, but really manipulating everyone as always. He was gone less than a year then completely exonerated in Rose's eyes. What a thing I had put that poor man through!

I was eighteen when I realised I was pregnant again. Greg was my brother's friend, but I had known him for years, which wasn't surprising given that everyone in Shannon knows everyone else. He lived in a house with Alan and another lad, while I stayed in Dublin on and off with Aunt Imelda. All I ever heard from Mom was that she missed Harry. She was like a broken record, but there's a draw to your home that you can't deny and so I started staying a day here and there in Shannon until I was splitting my time between the two places. Alan went to England around then, but Greg kept calling in. I definitely got on better with fellas than girls for a while, maybe because a lot of my friends were starting out with serious boyfriends and I didn't want anything to do with the rosy view they had and thought nothing of being so close to Greg. We'd lie in bed together, completely innocent, just listening to Nirvana and Depeche Mode and Lenny Kravitz. We'd be messing about, roaring with laughter – Rose was always sticking her head round the door, telling us off for even breathing. Anyway, it slowly developed into something else.

Harry might have been gone but my mother was still seeing him every Wednesday, coming back on the last bus and staying over on the Saturday. One time, she rang me on the Wednesday: 'I was wondering, do you think I could stay with your dad tonight?'

'Why the fuck are you asking me, Rose? Shall we do

a deal? You give me the code for the telephone and I can stay up all night calling my friends, running up your bill, and you can cosy up with Harry. That OK?'

The phone had been locked ever since he said we were using it too much, but she was so thick, I knew the code the first time I tried – 2580, the numbers running down in a little line on the keyboard. She got a payphone with a lock after that.

When Rose was gone at weekends, lots of people would be round the house, all drinking, and eventually, the inevitable happened with me and Greg. One night, there was just us in the house, months down the line, and I knew this was it. I still had to face the big one – having sex with a lad. He'd been in relationships before, but to my mind, I was a virgin. The same thing happened as it had with my last boyfriend: I got so far and then panicked. I couldn't do it, I just couldn't let that happen to me; I had no concept of sex being enjoyable or something for me, I just thought I'd have to endure it. It finally did happen when we had a water fight inside the house and my T-shirt got soaked.

'Look what you've gone and done! I'll have to go change this now.'

Such a cliché, but he offered to come and help me.

'Come on so,' I told him.

There was something much more natural about being together at that moment, upstairs, and I finally managed. All I can say is it wasn't that bad. There were no choirs of angels, no actual pleasure for me, and I did just lie there, but it was done – I'd managed. It was a relief, but it wasn't a revelation, just something you had to do. I really liked him, which was why I did it. If it had been down to me, I wouldn't have bothered.

Greg knew what had been done to me as a child. Everyone knew – but they didn't really know, if that makes sense? I certainly wasn't quiet about it, why should I be? It was Harry's shame, not mine. Alan would have told him to begin with, then my openness about Mom was clear to anyone. I'd get upset when she went off to him, not understanding why she stuck by that bastard, and so I would let off steam to Greg. No one ever picked away at what I was saying, no one ever looked at it in any detail or asked me if I needed anything. Abuse was a massive secret, people didn't talk about it, but I told everyone. I wanted to break barriers to do with testing people and pushing them as far as I could. I'd done nothing wrong, it was all him.

Why were the abused meant to feel bad when the abusers got away with it?

Greg and I started sleeping together on the Wednesday when Mom got back late and the Saturday while she was away. I can count how many times we had sex before I fell pregnant: eight. Eight times. We used no contraception – we thought we were invincible, as you do at that age.

I'd had no morning sickness with the first pregnancy, but with this baby, I knew even before I was late. I had my last period on 12th December 1993 and I know that for sure as it was my first ever concert. Greg had tickets for Depeche Mode in Dublin – there's even a recording for the gig where you can see him lifting me up onto the barrier, because I'm so tall you can clearly see me waving my hands about! – and I was walking on air. I started my period that evening when we got back and within a couple of weeks I knew. I had an erratic cycle, but this time I knew, I just knew within about a week of being late. On New Year's Day, it was obvious to me.

'Rose, I feel like I'm up the duff,' I told her boldly.

'What?'

'I feel like I'm pregnant.'

'What do you mean?'

'Well, what do you think I mean, you eejit? Is there something else I could mean when I say I think I'm pregnant?'

She was so excited – she probably thought it was a sign that our family could be this perfect fairy tale she'd always pretended it was. Greg was a bit dim about it too, which was fair enough as we'd hardly had sex and certainly hadn't planned for this. You had to be ten days late to go to the GP back then, there weren't any home pregnancy tests unless you paid a fortune – actually, looking back, maybe Carly had pinched the last one. While Rose waited outside, I took a urine sample into the doctor. At that time I was doing an electric assembly course and thought my life might start to get a bit better, but this could change everything. I was staring out the window when the doctor said, 'You're pregnant, Shaneda.' He had a look of doom on his face. 'Do you want me to tell your parents?' he said seriously.

'Are you kidding? My mother's outside planning the nursery – she's delighted.'

Rose was giddy when I told her, hugging me, which was the last thing I wanted. We went to the shopping centre to meet Greg and I can't really even remember his reaction, I just delivered my lines, told him that I was pregnant and that was that. There was nothing I really needed from him as my thought was that all men were useless bastards. He was only eighteen as well, we were just kids. And how did I feel? I wanted it – I wanted someone to love who loved me back. This baby was different as it wasn't Harry's, this wasn't a monster, this one would be human.

Being pregnant wasn't the only big change in my life. On Christmas Eve, Rose had asked if Harry could stay over for the night so that he would be there for Eve and Louise the next morning. I shrugged. I didn't want him there, of course I didn't, but I also didn't want to hear her whinging all day and just waiting for a chance to escape to him in their love nest. She's never done anything in her life but guilt me and this was no different.

Harry did stay that night, waltzing in bag and baggage, and he never moved back out again. He was like a different man. Alan and I cursed in front of him, he didn't react. We did whatever we wanted, he didn't rise to it. He was never in a mood, he was chilled – it was just another fake Harry, I reckoned. When he came back to the house, he never mentioned the abuse. Rose would still say how awful it was when she saw a storyline on TV – I don't know if she was oblivious or stupid or trying to hurt me or in denial. Probably a mixture of all four.

'Oh my God, would you look at that? That's just awful – how do people cope with such terrible things?'

I'd look at her and think, what is wrong with that woman? When I think about the whole picture, she did know. She couldn't act like she didn't know when she watched her stupid programmes because he had admitted it all. There were so many details and Harry had said it was all true. There was actually a letter he sent me when I left home in which he'd said all sorts:

I hope you're well – I've been thinking about you a lot.

(Have you, Harry? Well, isn't that nice?)

I'm so sorry about what happened.

(Ah sure, that makes it all fine.)

I'm going to therapy now.

(Are you? And do they know you're an evil bastard?)

I realise the destruction I've caused.

(Wouldn't it have been grand if you'd realised that when you were raping a little girl for years, Harry?)

I've changed, I'll be a better person.

(I'm not being harsh now, but it's a bit late, wouldn't you say? And, to be honest, I don't believe a fucking word of it.)

I worry about your future, Shan.

(So you should. I've had a bit of a time, really.)

Maybe you should get some counselling?

(Maybe you should fuck off?)

I'd told Mom all about that letter, she couldn't plead ignorance at any point. Despite the fact that Harry had admitted the abuse and the fact that he was in therapy, nothing was done. At one point, Mom was crying hysterically in her room and she showed me a letter to her at the start of that time he was away. He said that he was cutting all ties as it was for the best. They still seemed to believe they were Romeo and Juliet, acting like star-crossed lovers – the world was conspiring to keep them apart, their love was something that had to be fought for but it was worth it. Worth fighting for a paedophile who had raped his own daughter for years? My mother was some piece of work! I was lost in the midst of all this, no one considered what had been done to me: they had been destroyed, their journey ruined – why would I matter?

Rose told me he'd had a call to go into Henry Street Guard Station, about eight months after it had all come out.

'Are you going to take this to court?' she whined.

'No, I'm not – I don't want to talk about all this any more,' I told her and then I hung up.

The guards chatted to Dad and basically had a quiet word, marked his card off the record and did nothing else. All this was going round in my head when I first found out I was having the baby. This one wasn't his, but Rose was acting as if we were all perfect and all that 'stuff' was behind us.

A grandchild would show the world just how perfect the Dalys were.

CHAPTER 15

My Babies

———

I was so sick for a while, I couldn't even sit up straight without vomiting. Any time my feet hit the floor, I was sick. Any time I moved my head, I was sick. Nobody made a big deal out of it though.

I was always forward-thinking despite being brought up in such a backwater and there was no one, no one, who would make me feel this pregnancy was wrong in any way, shape or form. In January 1994, I made an instant decision that I didn't need Greg around for any of it.

'You're only with me because I'm pregnant, aren't you?' I said.

Before he had time to answer, I told him we were over. He was shell-shocked, broken-hearted for a week before I took him back – and that was us for ten happy years.

I always pushed and pushed and pushed people away though so it couldn't continue forever, I knew that.

I was sick until the May and felt that everything had changed while I had been in bed throwing up for five months. Lorraine and her partner Niall were moving to England, Donna went to Jersey, so did my other friend Jackie – lots of Irish people went there – another went to Germany and another to France. And I was still there with a baby.

I knew I wanted to move out and Harry had so much guilt, so much need to be seen as a good guy now, that he funded it. He gave us money for a deposit and took me to the shops, where I filled two trollies full of everything I needed, from salt and pepper pots to the most expensive pram I could find. It was like the old days when he would buy me anything for the look of it while being the shittiest dad in the world.

Time was moving on, I was getting bigger and it was time for the scan, but I didn't want it.

I'd convinced myself the baby was dead.

Or it was going to have Down's syndrome.

Or it would be stillborn.

Or it might die as soon as it was born.

Or, dear God, it would be a boy. I couldn't have that, I only wanted a girl.

Rose took me to my first scan but there was no way I would let her in: this was for me. What people don't realise is just how triggering all of that can be. There is growing awareness that the actual delivery of the baby can bring about so much that it makes victims of abuse have flashbacks, but I found the scan bad too. I had no idea they were going to squirt the cold gel on my tummy and that felt just like Harry ejaculating on me. I'm only just thinking that as I write this, I've never made the link before. I was the most naive teenager you could find. As I've said, I thought that babies were just blobs – although blobs that got bigger every month – until just before they were born, when they turned into real babies. When I looked at the screen and saw a fully formed baby, I was amazed.

Dear God, there was a baby in there!

When I saw that it was a real baby, moving, it made me roar with laughter. The sonographer shouted at me to stay still, but I couldn't work out what was going on, how could the baby be fully formed at twenty weeks? How could that be a baby that would grow rather than a pile of goo until the delivery?

That night, I was lying on the sofa watching films with Greg. I'd been so sick for five months that my stomach actually went in, there was no sticking-out bump.

'Stop that!' I shouted.

'What? What have I done?' he replied.

'Stop sticking your finger in my stomach!'

'I didn't! I'm not doing anything.'

Then I realised it was from the other side: it was my

baby kicking for the first time. I started creasing myself with laughter and Rose came downstairs, we'd woken everyone up with the commotion.

When I was ten days late, I was told I'd have to be induced. Rose and Harry dropped me off at the hospital and then fucked off to Kildare for a romantic five-day getaway. It was 25 September 1994 when I went in. I knew nothing and Greg wasn't going to be any use. To this day, I tell everyone what will happen when they go into hospital to have a baby because no one told me. I didn't know about enemas, or internals, or pessaries, or lying with my legs open while a stranger looked inside me; everything was so invasive and took me back to all of the abuse I'd been through. To be told to respond to demands and have no control was a nightmare, my body was taken over and just had things done to it. They tried to induce me for three whole days.

When Greg came in to see me on the day of the birth – finally – I didn't really want him there. The pain was so bad and it had been going on for so long. I knew I was dissociating from it all, from the waves I could see passing over my belly. Was this it? Off I went to the smoking room, where all the other mothers were. It's mad to think that's what it was like back then – smoking was just seen as normal and even after women had just had their babies, no one would bat an eyelid if they went off for a smoke as soon as they could.

'Here,' I asked them as one group, 'what's a contraction like?'

I swear they all stifled laughs at that point.

'What do *you* think they're like?' one of them asked me.

'I don't really know, but I've got this thing that feels like a balloon is inflating inside of me and trying to escape.'

'Then I think it's time to go tell a nurse,' she said.

All of my big plans went out the window. I'd said that I wasn't going to have pethidine, I wasn't going to have an epidural, I would do this all by myself, big brave Shaneda. Not now – I wanted everything I could get my hands on.

'You're only 2cm dilated, you've a long way to go.' The midwife gave me a sickly-sweet smile. 'One pain less is one pain closer to your baby.'

I did well not to tell her where to go, but when I was moved to the next room, I wasn't so well behaved. The new midwife in there patted my hand, saying, 'One pain less is one pain closer to your baby.'

'Jesus, you get taught to say that, don't you? You learn it in midwife school!' I roared, with a few expletives thrown in.

By the time Greg followed me in, he looked like he would collapse.

'It's time to push, Shaneda,' the midwife said.

From what I'd seen on TV, I thought that took hours, but they were telling me to get going. Greg was offered a chair to sit down at the business end – I think they were joking with him, but he was ready to faint so I sent him out for a cigarette. He had barely left the room when I was told the baby was in distress.

'You need to push properly now, Shaneda. You need to get this baby out, it doesn't want to be in there any more.'

It felt like seconds later and a lifetime later that someone said, 'It's a girl!'

'Let me see,' I cried. 'I need to check, I need to see all of her.'

'It's definitely a girl.'

'Then MOVE THE CORD!'

And there she was.

There was my Celina.

It was the best moment of my life, heartbreakingly emotional and perfect. Greg had missed it all, but I only had eyes for my little girl. Eight pounds five ounces of absolute joy, love I had never felt before. She was fat and wrinkly and mine.

I was horrifically sick within about an hour and so the midwives took Celina away for the night. When I got her back the next day, I was obsessed. I couldn't stop looking at her. No one was ever going to hurt her. This was my job forever – no one would touch her. I used to sing the Morrissey song, 'You're the One for Me, Fatty', to her, gazing at her perfect skin, her little feet, her perfect fingers. She could have had two heads and ten arms, she could have been the monster I'd always worried about, she would still have been my world. I knew I would always protect my baby but what I'd felt about needing to keep her safe during the pregnancy was nothing compared to what it was like after the birth.

Mom had demanded that I stay with her for two weeks to get used to the baby. I lasted one day before moving back to the flat with Greg. We were just kids – only nineteen – we slept when she slept and when she was lying, kicking her legs about, we played Mario Kart on the Nintendo. It was so easy-going, with just the three of us together, doting on her. A part of me had settled, something was right in my world. I was happy at that point, we didn't care what time she woke, it was all grand. I was determined not to fall into the trap of being a worn-down woman and sometimes I would pack up all her things and say to Greg, 'Right, take her out for the day – she's yours too.' I'd made sure she had my surname and when the nurse looked shocked, I stood my ground: 'I'm guaranteed to be around all her life but I'm not sure this fella will be – why wouldn't she have mine?'

We were just kids who happened to have a baby.

Harry was like a new man. No temper tantrums since he had got back – no nastiness, it was as if he'd had a personality transplant. I was in their house a lot and it seemed like we almost had a friendship. Looking back, that wasn't the case at all, he was still being a sneaky bastard and playing a part.

Celina had been taken into hospital when she was about four months old, on Christmas Night, as she had bronchiolitis from the damp in the flat (she's chronically asthmatic to this day), which made us move out to stay in Alan's flat for a bit. His girlfriend was pregnant and it wasn't long before she went back to her parents and he went to ours to try and save a bit of money before the baby came. I was put in the room on a camp bed with Celina, in a room I had to share with Louise too, while Alan got a room to himself. Rose was always obsessed with money and her eyes lit up at the prospect of being able to charge me £20 a week to stay, £20 a week for the baby, £20 if ever I wanted to go out with the girls for a night and £20 a week to look after her while I went back to work in a factory on the electronic assembly line. Everything with Rose was about money. After a while, I got the second dining room to have a bit more space once Celina was in her walker, moving around, but in all the time Harry was back in the house, it never felt like home. I wouldn't touch him even if I was passing something like the sauce bottle. I would extend my arm as far as I could or shove it across the table to him. He might seem changed to other people, but he still turned my stomach and I didn't trust him. Every now and again, I would get an involuntary shiver whenever I thought, *Urgh, my dad*. I didn't think specific things, I just got this weird quiver. He was never allowed to be alone with Celina.

He was a good enough father at that stage – or at least he made a great show of it. He was funny, he took me and Celina and Eve on trips and his temper seemed to have disappeared. I was prepared to draw a line under everything, never think of it again – so why was I still getting these responses which came out of nowhere? They were like body memories, reactions with a mind of their own. He never mentioned the past. He had turned into this new, much better dad, which, I suppose, looking back, was fair enough – he'd always been able to act a part.

Lorraine came back a month after Celina was born. She had been sending me the most beautiful clothes from Mothercare, a store we didn't have in Ireland – all frilly pink things. People used to stop me in the street to ask where they were from as all the girl babies were dressed in lemon or green back then, but I had these amazing outfits from England. Pink leggings, little shoes with ribbons, hats with bows – she was very spoilt and I spent every penny I had on her as well as having the fancy wardrobe from Lorraine.

I moved out when Celina was one, just to an apartment up the road, the two of us. Although I loved her to bits, being a mother didn't come naturally to me. There was once a radio programme on when I was at work, about mother-baby bonds, and lots of women rang in to say they loved their children but there was also something missing. I felt that way. I knew I didn't have the bond – until I moved out again. All I needed was one-on-one time with my little girl and it bloomed. I was obsessed with keeping her safe. She never had so much as a bruise on her. I did find it easier once she was a little person who was finding her own way, once her personality developed and our relationship definitely had that bond.

I fell pregnant again and thankfully only had nausea rather than the months of vomiting which came with my first. Foolishly – to me – I mentioned the abuse at one of my clinic appointments and before I knew what was happening, social workers appeared, telling me I needed to talk, telling me I needed counselling. But I thought I didn't need that at all and told my GP to get it stopped. I was terrified they would label me damaged and take my babies, that they would see it as something I had done wrong and decide I wasn't a fit mother.

Everything was different this time around as I knew what to expect with my pregnancy. I didn't panic over the scanning gel, I didn't fear the induction and I didn't even need an epidural as I was fully dilated within two hours and there was no time for it.

My boy was born in March 1997 when Celina was two and a half. He was 9lb 9oz and over two-foot long, the skinniest, scrawniest baby in the world. He needed a strong name. I'd been calling him Buster while he was inside and it was always important to me that my children weren't named after anyone in my family, which was hard given that there was such a huge gang of people. I went for Keith and it fitted him perfectly, my huge baby who everyone came in to see in hospital as they'd heard of this giant boy.

I did need another episiotomy and stitches, but that was a badge of honour – no way was I going to be telling people I'd had a baby that size without having to have stitches too! My bond with Keith was instant; he was put up beside my face instantly. I stroked him through the vernix, the goo that covered him, and I just flooded with love. I don't think I really knew what I had missed out on with Celina until I felt that rush. Her birth had been so traumatic and this one was a bit less terrifying. I didn't even mind having a boy. I had my girl and didn't mind what I got from this point on.

I was pregnant again in 1999 with my third baby, Steven, and was absolutely exhausted. I'd been very sick again, losing two stone during the pregnancy, and went back to stay at home. Rose went off to Dublin while I was there and I felt immediately antsy the moment she walked out the door. I didn't know what it was – something primal, some gut feeling. Alan was the only other one staying there and if he left the room, I felt a cold fear wash over me. Throughout 2000, the year Steven was born, I constantly felt that something wasn't right and early in 2001, I told Lorraine what was bothering me.

'This is the year something will happen with my dad. I don't know how I know but I just feel it.'

'What do you mean?'

'I don't really know, I just feel it.'

That was in the January.

I felt that he was getting nearer and nearer. Not just physically, but mentally too.

He was coming into my space.

Harry was coming back to hurt me.

CHAPTER 16

Groomed

It didn't matter that he was presenting himself as a new, better version of Harry Daly, there was something wrong. I know now that he was grooming me again. We went to see his sister one day and he kept insisting I have a drink. When I had one, he wanted me to have another. I had two and he wanted me to have more. He wasn't drinking though.

'No, I don't fancy it – that's more than enough,' I told him.

'Ah, go on, Shan,' he kept encouraging me. 'What's the harm after all?'

But there was harm, I sensed it.

Another day, we were coming back from visiting family and he stopped the car.

'I need a piss,' he said.

'Jesus, can't you wait? Just get on with it if you have to,' I sighed. I looked out of the side of the car when he got out and he was there. Just at my door, flies open and everything on display. There was no need for him to do that – any normal person who got caught short would have tried to be discreet, but he was being really obvious about it as close as he could get to me. That happened every time we were out. I felt it. He had plans. And he was talking about the past.

'Will you ever forgive me for what I did to you?' he asked one day, again in the car.

I could feel tension in my body immediately. 'I've forgiven you,' I snapped. 'Actually, I've forgotten.' I just wanted him to shut up, I just wanted out of the car.

'You must have been so scared, Shan, when you came in, knowing that I was going to molest you.'

'It doesn't matter. We don't need to talk about this now.'

But he kept on, niggling at me, as I panicked, thinking something else was going to happen.

When I got back, I went straight upstairs to my cousin Jeff, who was staying there for some reason I can't remember. Shaking him, I told him that Harry had been weird in the car. None of my family ever knew how to respond to me when I raised it, but he did leave his door open that night and listened out. I didn't want to tell Greg, I wanted to keep that away from him.

I knew something was coming. Harry was getting bolder even, raising the stakes of things – he was testing the water. One Saturday, I was upstairs in his room where he kept the computer. I wanted to get a Destiny's Child ringtone downloaded onto my mobile phone – that was the height of technology back then! There was no one in the house apart from me and him as the kids were with Greg at their grandparents. I heard the creaking of the stairs and froze.

There he was. There was Harry – and I was in his room. He sat down beside me on the little stool, squeezing close as I looked at the computer screen. His hand went around my waist and I couldn't move. He put his hand completely up into my bra and fondled my breast. I said nothing. He kept his hand there for about ten minutes, just feeling me, not doing anything else. I knew he was checking whether I would do anything and I didn't.

'I want to go home,' I whispered.

When the phone went that night, I was terrified at the thought it would be him but it was Rose.

'Are you coming up for dinner tomorrow for Greg's birthday?' she asked.

'No,' I said shortly.

Her whining started. 'Oh, but it'll be a shame if you don't. The kids will miss you. Greg will want to come. Shan, go on, just do it, where's the bother?' On and on she went, her voice like nails down a blackboard to me before I finally agreed to go.

As soon as we got there, Harry was at my side.

'Do you want to go upstairs and look at those things?' he asked, quietly.

'What "things"? What the fuck are you talking about?'

'The things on the computer.'

'The ringtones?'

'Whatever – do you want to?'

He kept asking, so I finally relented and said, 'Come on, Greg, come upstairs and I'll sort out the music for my phone.' He looked at me, totally confused, and followed me up. No sooner were we in there than Harry told him to get back downstairs.

'Stick on the kettle there, Greg, and make us a cup of tea.'

Greg left and I was instantly taken back to all the times I'd had to make cups of tea for Dad. I sat down at the computer and he went to do it again, I pushed his hand away and he said, 'What's wrong?'

'Don't! Just don't!'

'You can't let me do it one day and not the next,' he said as if I wasn't playing a game fairly.

I stood up. 'Do you want to fucking bet?'

The stool went flying behind me, I shouted to Greg to get the kids as we were leaving and I don't remember anything else until we got back to our house. I wouldn't tell Greg what had happened as I didn't want to spoil his birthday but I made a promise to myself that as soon as the clock struck midnight and it was a normal day, I would. We were both lying in bed, in the dark – which was how it needed to be, I never wanted to see the reaction on anyone else's face when I told them things like this.

'I don't want you to do anything,' I said. 'I just want you to know.'

He went mental, saying he was going to kill my father, that he would smash all the windows at their house, I begged him not to because my sisters were there.

The next day, I decided I'd tell Rose. Harry was texting me and leaving messages all day, pretending that he was concerned about how I was, acting like the good father rather than the absolute horror he was. I went up to the house, but Rose was babysitting the kids of one of her friends and I didn't want to bring upset into that. The next day, there was someone else in the house. I couldn't sleep, I couldn't eat – I had to tell her. She'd forgiven him everything else but this would surely make her see that it had all been a lie, that he had just been biding his time.

On that day, Greg phoned him.

'You're a dirty pervert! You're a fucking freak, Harry Daly!' he screamed.

The truth was, I was delighted someone was finally openly on my side. Harry still kept phoning me and I answered on the millionth call.

'You need to tell Rose what you did. Do you hear me, Harry? You have to tell your wife.'

'Yeah, OK,' he answered as if I'd just asked him to pass on a message about going to the shops.

She called me back instantly: 'I'll be down in five minutes.'

I don't have much memory of it all, but some of her words do stick in my mind.

I can't believe he's done this again.

He promised me that he wouldn't touch you any more.

Why has he done this? Why?

I trusted him.

She was crying, as usual, but I did feel something had changed. That was it. She couldn't ignore this.

But she could.

Greg took a week off work and I stayed in bed. I felt like I was dying. It actually felt far worse than the first time because it was reigniting all the feelings I had locked away. I found it so hard to get over – and it finished me and Greg a few years later. He had seen me for so many years getting on with life that this was a shock to him. I was so angry as well about Rose staying with Harry, about them being a cosy couple again. My mood was all over the place and Harry wouldn't leave me alone, phoning me, texting me, asking how life was, how the kids were, as if he hadn't done any of it.

I never saw Harry or Rose again until 2006 because I had this sense that he had opened the floodgates again. He would keep pushing and pushing until I gave in and it all went back to how it was. When I was a little girl, I'd feared that I would end up married to him, that I would have children by him, that it would go on forever. Even if I escaped and married someone else, he would still do it. Now that I was a mother of three children, he still thought he had the right to my body. People think of 'child' abuse – I was an adult and he was still violating me. It brought up all the stuff I had never dealt with and put me in such a bad place.

I was never the same after my father assaulted me. He was texting me all the time, it was constant and I felt like I'd never get away from him. In 2003, I split with Greg because of it. I just needed to be alone with my children. He moved a few minutes away from us and took them a couple of hours a week and every second weekend. When it was just me and the kids, I learned how to love myself for the first time in my life. I was really happy once I saw the value of my own company and started to care for myself. I didn't realise it was happening, but it did. I'd never been on my own before. It didn't stop me being over-protective with Celina though. I wouldn't let her wear nightdresses, it had to be pyjamas. She wouldn't have summer dresses, it had to be leggings. I had to make sure there was no easy access for anyone to get near her. She was always in my line of vision and there were very few people I would leave her with. When Lorraine took her to the beach, there were rules.

'You have to draw a square in the sand and don't let her across the lines. You have to realise there are fifty kids on the beach and they all look the same. You might think you can see her, but you can't be sure unless she's right next to you.' I was so paranoid about my daughter going missing, I even did the square in the sand when I was the only one looking after her.

I was a kind mother, I loved them with all my heart – I read them stories all the time as I wanted to pass on my love of reading, I saved money so they always had the latest Disney video when it came out. In winter, they'd come home from school and nursery to a roaring fire and all their cosy clothes warm, waiting for them, with cuddles galore. It was hard being a single parent but Greg was a good dad when he could be but he worked full-time so was limited in the time he could spend with them. I had no interest whatsoever in being with anybody else. Every so often I went out with Lorraine and other girls and I happened to go back to meet one of them one night and a fella walked in the room and said, 'Here, I know you.'

That was Jack.

We fell into being together. I didn't believe in having different children with different dads – it was sick and wrong in my mind. Kids with twenty different grandparents didn't know what was going on and that wouldn't be my life. Of course, I ended up pregnant. I was devastated. Jack was delighted. I was terrified of childbirth again.

Steven's shoulder had got stuck when he came out and the afterpains were horrific. I was in shock postnatally, a silver blanket over me, my blood pressure crashing – I did *not* want to go through that again. I loved my son even before I met him, but it had been so hard.

I went for the scan with fear in my heart because I'd been bleeding, but when they showed me the screen, everything seemed fine: there was a heartbeart and a little blob which changed my mind. Of course, I wanted the baby – of course I did.

When the bleeding got even worse the next week, I knew that no little one could survive that. The sonographer said the words no woman wants to hear: 'I'm so sorry, Shaneda, your baby has died.'

Died? How could that be? How could it still be in me but not alive? I went around for a week waiting for the miscarriage to start, bluntly telling everyone, 'There's a dead baby inside me.' I'd never heard of missed miscarriage before, of how common it was, and assumed it was due to the abortion all those years ago. On the Monday, I was due to go into the maternity unit to have a D&C, but driving to Jack's parents on the Saturday, I felt like I was in the height of labour, like I needed gas, it was so bad. I went into the supermarket to get pads, there was this sensation of a wave of pain and then it passed.

I went to the toilet as soon as we got to their house and all I heard was *plop, plop, plop*. I couldn't look, I just flushed the toilet and walked out. Just like the abortion all over again. I felt a failure; my body had let me down. I was about eleven weeks. I'll always remember the day I lost that baby and the day it should have been born. I lost it on 11 November 2004, the same day three years ago when Harry had last assaulted me.

Time passed and a few years later, Jack and I welcomed a baby boy. The calls and messages and texts from Harry were still going on. I made a pact with God or whoever, whatever, that if this baby survived, I'd be strong enough never to have any contact with Harry ever again.

I was in a shopping centre in Limerick with Jack one day in 2006 when I saw Harry for the first time since he had assaulted me. I recognised him by his walk, then, whatever way I looked, I knew it was definitely him. We went past and Jack said, 'Was that your dad?'

'Yeah, but I'm not leaving. Let *him* leave,' I told him.

Shaking from head to toe, I managed to get to the other end of the mall. I needed to get back to the car but I honestly didn't want to see him, so walked around the outside perimeter of the shopping centre to the car park rather than run the risk.

A few years after, I had my second daughter. I looked at Jack holding her just after she was born and there was such pure love coming from him that I thought for the first time, *did my parents ever look at me that way?* He was besotted with her from the start and my head was spinning. *When did Harry stop thinking of me as his child? When did he start to think of me as something that was just there for him to abuse and rape? Did he still think of himself as my father while he did that? When did his love for me change from the right type to something so evil? Had he ever felt the right way, the way a father should for his little girl? When did my mother decide it was OK for her baby to be raped every day?*

The thoughts wouldn't stop.

I'd had postnatal depression with my youngest boy, but by the time it was acknowledged, Jack was helping more and I didn't need medication. On 11 November, the date that always came back to bite me, the postnatal midwife kept asking me if I was alright. I said I was, but on the way home, I just wanted to disappear as there was such an overwhelming feeling of hopelessness. I got home and burst out crying.

'You can't go through this again,' said Jack. 'Get in the car and we'll bring you to the doctor.' I was put on antidepressants and they did help, although I was numbed a lot. I also got some counselling and at the same time, found out that my sister Eve was pregnant.

'You need to do something about this,' I impressed upon the counsellor. 'He abused me for years, now she's pregnant, waiting on a little girl and stuck in that house – it's not right.'

I pushed it as much as I could, but without her reporting

anything, no one would act. It seemed as if things were coming up all of the time. My childhood, right up until I was seventeen, was in my mind constantly. I was getting shakes and shivers out of nowhere and I couldn't seem to drag my mind away from my past. I began to think that, for the first time, I wanted to do something about it at some point, to get Harry to pay. Had Harry even loved me – or had he just seen me as something to be used from the start?

Six months after my first batch of antidepressants, I was back to get a repeat prescription. As the GP wrote the script, I had a flash of awareness.

'I don't think I have post-natal depression actually,' I told him. 'I have depression full stop and I've had it for years. When you have babies, it's harder to push feelings back, as the emotions are all sitting so close to the surface. Do you remember I told you before that I'd been sexually abused?'

He nodded.

'Well, it was my dad.'

He was Harry's GP too.

Celina did have a relationship with her grandparents but it was on my terms. She could only be dropped off by me or Jack, or picked up by Rose, and Harry had to be out at work when she was there. He was to have no contact with her whatsoever, I couldn't risk it. She had to be with one of my sisters at all times. As she was getting older –

fifteen when her little sister was born – she was bolder and wanted to know why there was no love lost between me and my parents.

'What is it? Why doesn't Mom talk to Grandad?' she constantly asked my cousins, who reported back to me. They had been warned to gloss over it, not to tell her a word of the real reason. I wanted her protected. But she wouldn't let it lie and one day said to one of them, Karen, 'I know, I know why she doesn't talk to him.'

'Do you? Well, you tell me – what do you think it is?'

'I think he did something to my mom.'

When that came out, when Karen phoned to warn me, my heart sank: 'Come over, Shaneda, you need to deal with this.'

I got to Karen's house as quickly as I could. Celina was on her sofa.

'What's wrong?' I asked. 'Is this all about why I don't talk to your grandparents?'

'He did something to you, didn't he? Grandad did something to you.'

I looked at her and my heart sank. I'd never wanted her to know all of that, never wanted her to be exposed to it, but she was almost a woman now and I didn't want the lies to continue, even if they were just by avoiding the subject.

'He did,' I nodded.

'I knew it,' she replied. 'I knew this wasn't about money

because it feels too big. It feels like something is being kept from me. What did he do?'

I told her that he had abused me, without going into too much detail. I certainly never told her it was every day, often more than once a day, for so long. Naturally, she was upset and I reassured her and hugged her, then realised that I needed to tell Eve and see what her reaction was. She adored me – after all, I'd practically raised her – but she adored our parents too. It was 50/50 who she would believe.

'I need to tell you something, Eve, you know why me and Dad don't talk?'

'Yeah, it's over money.'

'It's nothing to do with money, it's something much more serious.'

'Is it because he used to beat you?'

'No – it's something more serious than that.'

Her face was an explosion of expressions before she settled on fury as the realisation came to her of what I meant. 'What? The devious bastard!' She was on the phone to him instantly. 'You dirty rapist!' she screamed. 'You fucking paedophile!' She was calling him everything under the sun.

There was nothing else I could do. Eve knew now and I was fully aware that it would be the talk of the family – again – soon. It was such a beautiful day. I remember hanging out of the window, enjoying the sun, when my phone rang.

Rose.

There was no preamble.

'Your father just wants to know – are you pressing charges?'

'No, but you tell him that he's done ever thinking he'll be back in my life.'

I got off the phone and sent a long text to her, I was sick of her living in La La Land. It was along the lines of:

Your husband is a rapist. He's raped me all my life. You don't even care – you keep going back to him, you keep choosing him. He had me in your bed while you were giving birth to Louise. Every time you kiss him, think of what that filthy mouth has done to your child, to his own daughter.

I went into so much detail, really disgusting things, but I wanted her to feel a sliver of the pain I felt.

Her next call was hysterical.

'I never knew it was that bad,' she sobbed.

'Are you kidding? I TOLD you!'

This was her reality, I hoped. As I sat on the windowsill, I felt quite calm, the sun shining on me, safe in my own home, and I realised something: I was done.

And I was just starting.

CHAPTER 17

All of It

Harry Daly had taken enough from me and Rose needed to know the truth; everyone needed to know the truth. I closed the window and made one more call. To the cop shop.

'Hi, I'd like to make an appointment, please. I want to come in and talk about being sexually abused.'

'When was it?'

'When I was a child.'

'Come down at 9 o'clock in the morning, we'll be waiting for you.'

How simple was that? How easy to set something in motion that would change everything?

The next morning, off I went. I'd told no one where I was going – seven hours of evidence later, my phone was hopping. My friend Aoife had called to the house and asked Celina if I was there.

'No, and I don't know where she is.'

'Is Shaneda's little one with you?' When Celina told her she was, Aoife started driving around as she said she knew something was wrong just from that. If I didn't have the little one, she said the only reason would be that I was in the cop shop. I had never talked to her in depth about the abuse but she knew me better than anyone. It might have been a leap for someone else to surmise where I was, but not her – she could read me like a book and had put everything together.

The cops told me they'd had a call from one of my friends, asking if I was there.

'You can tell her, I don't care.'

Within minutes, Jack called to ask where I was.

'In the guard station, making a statement.'

'Jesus! Come home when you're ready.'

Seven hours the first day

Six hours the next day.

Two hours each for all of the others.

I want to put my statement in here to show others what is asked of them – all of us who take that step are walking into the unknown. You will have to be stronger than you ever thought possible, but you can do it.

And this is how …

Statement of Shaneda Daly of Shannon, Co. Clare
Occupation: Housewife.
Date of Birth: 24/3/75

Taken on 16/7/10 at Shannon Garda Station

*I hereby declare that this statement is true to the
best of my knowledge and belief and that I make it
knowing that if it is tendered in evidence I will be
liable to prosecution if I state in it anything which I
know to be false or do not believe to be true.*

*Today the 16th of July 2010 I have come to
Shannon Garda Station to report abuse from the
age of 4 to 17 years by my father, Harry Daly. This
abuse was of a sexual nature. The first memory I
have of the abuse was when we lived in Ballymun,
Dublin. I was approximately four or five years of
age. The first time it happened my father asked
me to lie on the couch with him. I was in front of
him under a blanket. I remember it was a leather
couch. We were watching television at the time.
My father then put his hand into my panties and
started rubbing my vaginal area on the outside. I
remember this happening on numerous occasions.
I remember when my aunt used to stay over with
us in Ballymun, I remember telling her to sleep on
the outside of the bed because I knew my father*

*wouldn't come near me if she was on the outside.
My father was a prison officer in Mountjoy Prison
at the time.*

*We then moved from Ballymun to Limerick in
1982. I was approximately seven years old. It was
myself, my mother and father and my brother Alan
who lived at this address. We moved into a house
in Limerick City for a few weeks. It was prison
officer accommodation. I remember him touching
me at the address. He was lying on the bed under
the blankets and I was standing next to him
wearing a nightdress. He was touching my vagina
on the outside. It happened a couple of times
after that.*

*We then moved to Caherdavin, where we lived
for four or five months. I remember I was in
second class at Caherdavin school because of the
nuns. I remember the nuns didn't like my Dublin
accent. I also remember that my mother announced
she was pregnant at that house with my sister
Louise. I don't really remember him touching me
at this house. I was always outside, playing with
my friends. I remember learning how to cycle my
bike there.*

*We then moved to [a house in] Limerick.
I was approximately eight or nine years old when
I lived at this address. My sister Louise was born*

when we lived at this address. The touching continued at this address for a couple of months. The night my sister Louise was born on the 3rd of May 1983 was the first time my father got me to touch him. I remember being in his bed and he caught my hand and showed me how to masturbate him by putting his hand over mine and rubbing his penis up and down. I remember feeling the wetness so he must have ejaculated.

He usually used to come into my bedroom early in the morning before he went to work. I would be lying in bed pretending to be asleep and he would put his hand and feel my vaginal area. This continued on a regular basis. The masturbation happened two or three times when my mother was in hospital having my sister Louise. During the summer holidays of 1984, myself, Alan, Louise and my mother moved to Co. Kildare to my grandmother's house. My dad stayed in Limerick for work but used to visit at the weekends. The reason we went to Kildare was because my parents were trying to buy a house at O'Callaghan's Mills, Co. Clare. While we were living at my grandmother's, we all used to stay in a bedroom on the third floor. I remember my mom asking me to bring tea up to my dad when he was staying over in the morning time. He

*used to make me masturbate him while he was
lying in bed and I was standing at the side of the
bed in my nightdress. And sometimes he would
touch my vagina. This happened every weekend
morning he came to stay. I think it was September
when we moved to O'Callaghan's Mills. I
attended fourth class at the primary school there
for a bit. I was nine years old when I was living at
O'Callaghan's Mills.*

*I remember on one occasion I was in the bath
and my dad was washing me and he penetrated
my vagina with his fingers. I remember starting
to cry and my mom coming into the bathroom
and asking what was wrong. My dad told her I
got soap in my eyes. At night-time, my father used
to watch television in his bedroom and he would
look to have his supper or a cup of tea brought
to him. He always asked me. I remember at this
stage my father used to penetrate my vagina with
his fingers. He used to be lying on the bed wearing
underwear, I used to be fully clothed. Sometimes
he would get my hand and put it on his penis and
make me masturbate him. I felt pressured to do
it. Sometimes I'd move my hand away and he put
it back on his penis. It was never violent. It was
an everyday event at the address in O'Callaghan's
Mills. It usually happened in the evening times.*

*I remember moving to [a different] primary
school after the Easter holidays for the rest of
fourth class and all of fifth class and a few weeks of
sixth class. I would have been aged approximately
nine years to eleven years during this period.
Between the years of 1985–1986 we were living [in]
Raheen at this time. I know that it was the Raheen
address we were living at this time because we got
a new video recorder and the remote control was
attached to the machine by a cord. My mother
Rose Daly used to work at the Limerick Regional
Hospital as a cleaner from about 5pm–8pm during
the week. My brother Alan was approximately nine
years and sister Louise was two years at the time.
They would normally be in bed when my mother
was at work. They'd normally go to bed at about
5pm. It was then my father started putting on
pornography for me to watch with him. He showed
me from the video how to perform oral sex and
then I'd have to perform it on him. He used to be
naked when we were watching the pornography.
He would be holding his penis and making me put
his penis in my mouth. He didn't ejaculate the first
time he made me perform oral sex on him. This
happened nearly every night. He used to perform
oral sex on me too. I used to tell him I didn't want
to do it but he used to say, 'Come on, it's OK.'*

I remember another incident while living at the house in Raheen. I remember lying on the carpet on the floor in the living room and my father was lying on top of me. We were both naked. I can't remember if he undressed me or not. I remember telling him, 'Stop, it hurts.' He was having sexual intercourse with me at this time. I'm not sure if this was the first time that I had sexual intercourse with my father. I do not remember any bleeding. I do remember it happened after this on numerous occasions. It was usually when my mom was at work. He would be in the bath and he would call me in and make me sit on top of him. He would tell me to get undressed and get in. It would be full intercourse and he would ejaculate. After it was finished, he would tell me to get dressed and go to bed.

I was not on any contraception at this time and my father did not use any condoms. I got my period when I was nearly 14 years old when I was living in Shannon. This (the abuse) was a regular occurrence in the Raheen house. It would happen nearly every night. I was 11 years old when we moved to Shannon because I remember celebrating my 12th birthday as I got a parka jacket for my 12th birthday. We lived in Drumgeely Hill from October–March 1986–1987 and I do not

*remember any incidents occurring at this address.
We then moved. I felt this (next) house was the
House of Doom, there was no escape from him.
Every morning, he would come into my bedroom
before work and put his hand under the blanket
and into my pants and put his hand on my vagina
and penetrate it with his fingers. I used to always
pretend I was asleep. My father became more
daring. He would get me to bend over the banister
and look out for anybody coming. My mom, Alan
and Louise would be downstairs. He would then
penetrate my vagina from behind me with his penis.*

*I remember when I was about 14 years I was in
the sitting room with him and he pinned me to the
floor by putting his knees on my upper arms and
he ejaculated on my face because he was always
asking me to swallow his semen and I never would.
I remember this was a particularly humiliating
experience and he was violent but I was not
afraid of him. On my 13th birthday until my 17th
birthday, I used to always ask him could this be the
end of it because I was getting too old. He'd say
(yes) but it would start the next day again. He said
when I learned to enjoy it then it would stop. At
this stage when there was an incident it would be
sexual intercourse.*

My dad used to organise camping trips from

when I was 13 years old. There would be myself, my brother Alan, my dad and myself and Alan would bring one friend along each. We went to Castle Lough and Curragh Chase on one occasion. We would all stay in the one tent. We all had our own sleeping bags. He would get me to lie beside him so I would masturbate him while all the others were asleep. We would both be fully clothed. He never touched me in the tent. I remember one night when I was about 15 years old. Myself, my dad and my friends went camping at Castle Lough. My dad provided us with bottles of Budweiser and we spent about three or four nights there. On the first night he was trying to get me to go out to the car to masturbate him but I told him, 'no,' and went back into the tent. Another night he tried to call me, I told Lorraine to tell him I was asleep. I remember another night myself and my dad were parked in the old viewing area at Shannon Airport. He was asking me if a fella attacked me, what would I do? I replied I'd kill him. I was about 15 years old at the time. It was 1990. He then became very aggressive. He came towards me on the passenger seat, using his elbows and his body weight to pin me down. I told him to, 'Fuck off, get off me,' but he didn't and he had sexual intercourse with me. He penetrated my vagina with his penis. He ejaculated on the occasion.

Whenever I was in the car with him, he would get me to masturbate him. He would always have a hole, cut/rip in his left pocket and he would make me put my hand in his pocket while driving. He used to drive a Ford Granada car. On trips to Dublin, he would pull the car to the side of the dual carriageway and penetrate my vagina with his penis. This happened until I was 17 years old. When my dad went to collect Alan, he would ask me to come along and he would drive to Cratloe, an area known as the Golf Balls. There he used to pull down my clothes and penetrate my vagina with his penis. It usually happened either in the passenger seat or outside the car. These were also regular occurrences until I was nearly 18 years. When I was 14 years or 15 years, my dad would organise a day rock climbing or orienteering in Cratloe or Silvermines for me and my brother Alan. My dad would get Alan to go away and look for something and then my dad would have sex with me. It was usually up against a tree. We would both be still clothed but our trousers would be down and he would be penetrating my vagina with his penis.

My dad would ask me to call my friend to my house when I was having a bath so she could look after my sister Eve. Dad told me after that he felt her boob or felt her vagina. Down through the years, my father was extremely violent towards me and my brother Alan, he used to beat us with a bamboo stick, belt, slippers, hands, fists and feet. He used to deprive us of food. He was a control freak about time keeping. I was never afraid of him though. I moved out of home when I was 17 years old in October 1992. I moved back home in December 1992 on Christmas week. On Christmas morning, my dad pushed me against the breakfast counter and tried to feel me up but I pushed him away and I went to bed. I was woken up at lunchtime and he was sitting at the side of my bed, trying to put his hands into my pants. I started roaring, calling my mother and telling him to fuck off. He went running out of the room. I moved out of the house the next day again.

In January 1993 I came to Shannon Garda Station after having a row with my brother, Alan. I told the guard I wanted to press charges against Alan for hitting me. I then said I wanted to press charges against my dad for abuse and rape. I never made a statement in respect of this. My mother found out about the abuse when she came to the Garda Station to collect Alan. The next day my mother came to my house to ask me to ring my father in her presence and ask him had he been at

*my sisters, Louise and Eve. He said no, it was only
me. My mother was on another phone listening
to the conversation. He apologised to me on the
phone. I asked him why he did it and he said that
I was always his favourite and his princess. He
moved out of the house that evening.*

*In February 1993 I moved to my aunt Imelda
Rooney's house in Layland, Clondalkin, Dublin.
I stayed there for four or five months and she was
aware of what had happened. The first person I
ever told about the abuse was Carly [x] of [x] on
a night out in January 1993. I think it was the
same night I ended up in the Garda Station with
my brother. My dad returned to the house on
Christmas Eve 1993 and everything was forgotten
by everybody else.*

*Everything was fine until I was 26 years old.
We maintained a good relationship from when
I was 18 years to 26 years old. On the 10th
November 2001, I was in my dad's house using
his computer when he put his arm around me, put
it up my top and inside my bra. I said nothing and
after a few minutes I said, 'I want to go home,'
and he dropped me home. He said nothing either.
The next day I was in his house again on the
computer when he tried to put his hand up my
top. When I told him, 'No,' he said, 'You can't*

let me do it one day and not the next.' I stood up and said, 'You want to fucking bet?' I left and have never seen him since. Prior to this incident on 31st October 2001 we were coming back from Homebase in Dublin when my dad brought up a conversation about the abuse and asked me could I ever forgive him. I said ya because I felt uncomfortable because we were in the car in the middle of nowhere. He also brought up the conversation about the time he violently assaulted me at the view area in the airport. I had totally forgotten about this incident until he mentioned it and then it all fully came back.

I also remember when I was 15 years old, he used to get me to dress up in my mother's underwear, a white body suit and stockings prior to having sexual intercourse in his bedroom at Cluain Airne. Also, at times I would be talking to my friends out the window because I was grounded a lot. My dad would then penetrate my vagina from behind with his penis. This happened on several occasions. I think my dad got counselling about the abuse back in 1993. He sent me three letters during summer 1993 apologising that it wasn't my fault and I should get counselling myself. The reason I didn't report the abuse until now is because I felt no one was on my side and they would all prefer if I shut up about it and left it alone. The reason I'm reporting it now is that my daughter worked out why I don't speak to my father and my sister Eve recently had a baby girl and she recently moved back in with my parents. I have explained to my daughter Celina and sister Eve about everything that happened. Two weeks ago, I sent my mother a message detailing what he had done to me. She rang apologising and said she had kicked him out of the house.

I would also like to add that in March 1993 a note was put through the letter box at my parents' house that said, 'Get Dirty Harry out.'

I also want to add that my father pressured me to go on the contraceptive pill after my period started when I was nearly 14 years old.

This statement has been read over to me and is correct.

And there you have it. It was there in black-and-white. I'd started the ball rolling and there was no turning back.

CHAPTER 18

Admit the Crime

———

I had two guards, Suzanne and Lindsey, who were absolutely brilliant. One of them took me on fag breaks with her, I got tea and food whenever I wanted it – they were faultless. I was there to do a job, it was the only way I could apologise to my daughter for keeping that secret.

It was a normal interview room, with a chair bolted to the ground, two chairs opposite me for the cops and a boring table between us. They were both in uniform but they said if ever they called to my house, they would be in normal clothes. They were both trained in historical sexual abuse and they did their job well, however, I was an open book anyway and they didn't need to press me for anything.

My next statement went into more detail:

I wish to make an additional statement as I can recall more details of the abuse. I remember when I was 13 or 14 years old my dad asked me, 'did I remember the first time anything had happened between us?' I said, 'ya it was the time of the sitting room in Ballymun,' and he said, 'no, do you not remember the first time was in the bathroom in Ballymun?' I recalled the occasion he was on about when I had been rubbing soap into his chest hair. I was not in the bath with him. It would be normal for myself and Alan to be in and out of the bathroom when he was having a bath. I was rubbing soap into his chest which was a normal occurrence when I asked what was that and pointed down. He said it was his penis. He told me I could rub soap onto it, which I did for a few minutes and then I stopped. In Cluain Airne it would be a regular occurrence while I was in the bath for him to unlock the door from the outside with a coin or a knife or a key. Then he'd come in and he would be either touching my breasts or my vagina or inserting his fingers into my vagina while masturbating himself. This would have happened two or three times a week.

You have asked me to clarify about the bath incidents that occurred in relation to Raheen. He would call me into the bathroom while he was in the bath and tell me to undress and get into the bath. He would be already in the bath with no clothes on. He would get me to stand up near his face and he would perform oral sex on me and he would get me to sit down on his erect penis. He would be moving me up and down with his hands. He would have both hands on my waist. This would happen a couple of times a week. The oral sex began at Raheen. He'd make me do it to him and he would do it to me. This would normally happen before he would have sexual intercourse with me.

I remember one time me and Alan were playing hide and seek and my dad got me to hide under the quilt on his bed between his legs. My first recollection of having sex was in Raheen and it mostly happened downstairs in the sitting room and it would happen about twice a week. In relation to the abuse at Cluain Airne I have been asked to further clarify about my dad coming into my room every morning before work. He used to put his hand into my pants and insert his fingers inside me. I used to try and tie the elastic on my leggings so he couldn't get near me. He would just rub me then outside my clothes.

I recall an incident where I was lying on the couch with my father in Cluain Airne. He was lying behind me and I was wearing a nightdress and panties. He had his hand inside my pants; he was rubbing around my vaginal area. I remember 'Starman' was on TV. My mother walked into the sitting room unexpectedly. He then pulled his hand out really quick and then covered me with my nightdress. I pretended to be asleep. I remember my mother said to my father, 'What's she doing there? She should be in bed.' She then called me and said, 'Come on, Shan, up to bed.'

I've been further asked to clarify the incidents at the window in my first statement. I remember I'd be hanging out my bedroom window talking to my friends. My bedroom was at the front of the house. He would come up behind me and either perform oral sex on me or insert his fingers in my vagina. We used to have net curtains up and my friends couldn't see him.

I remember another time he got a brunch ice pop and spread it on his penis and then got me to lick it off. This happened in his bedroom in Cluain Airne two or three times when I was around 15 years old. The safety chain was always on the door in Cluain Airne so my mother couldn't come into the house without him knowing. In Cluain Airne he used to get me to sit next to him on the couch, he'd be sitting under a quilt and he would get me to masturbate him. There would have been other people there. Louise or Alan would be sitting on the floor but they wouldn't notice anything. I recall my dad telling me that he had touched my friend's breast on purpose and that he placed his mouth on her vagina through her jeans. She stopped calling after that for a long time. We never spoke about it to each other. I remember my dad came up to Dublin to collect me from my aunt's house. That friend had come with him for the spin. On the way back, she fell asleep in the back of the car and my dad kept on trying to place my hand on his exposed penis to get me to masturbate him. I was 14 years old at the time. This was July 1989.

I want to add that I became sexually active when I was 15 years old with a boy I met. My father had been at me since my period started to go on the contraceptive pill. I told my mother I wanted to go on the pill and she got it for me. I remember my dad used to tell me to clean my vaginal area after we had sex to try and get rid of the sperm. I moved out of home in October or November 1992. That night was the last night my dad had sex with me and I did not have sex with anybody in the period in between. I discovered I was pregnant in December 1992. A friend arranged for me to meet someone in Dublin. She brought me

*to a woman who examined my stomach and said
she reckoned I was 13 to 14 weeks pregnant. I was
saying I didn't want it and she gave me tablets. I
had to take them at two different times, I think it
was a day apart. As a result, I had a miscarriage. I
do not know who this woman was or her address.*

*I remember giving a computer to my friend x
that my dad had given to me. She told me that
when she hooked it up to the internet a load of
child pornography, photographs and emails came
up on the screen. She told me some of the emails
were from an American woman. I never looked at
the computer or the images and I told x to do what
she wants with it. The reason x told me about the
images was because I was warning her about the
dangers of the internet because my sister Louise
had been on the family computer when an image of
a child being raped had popped up on the screen.
This happened about six years ago. My mother
told me about it. This happened in Cluain Airne.*

*One time myself, my dad, Alan [and the Smiths]
went camping. My dad told me after that he had
purposely exposed himself in the tent while he had
a towel around him after swimming. X told me
about it afterwards. She was slagging me about it.*

*My mom told me one day my dad was very
upset. I asked her why and she said either his*

psychiatrist or physiologist (sic) told him that he was a pervert. I remember my partner at the time told me that he had [. . .] called him a pervert and a sicko down the phone. This took place after the time he felt my boob when I was 26 years old.

This statement has been read over to me and is correct.

There had been a story in one of the papers I had read the year before which said the highest number of charges in Ireland was 103 against the father who abused his children while they were in care. I remember saying to one of the guards, 'I would blow that number out of the water.' I'd said it flippantly but now I was facing the reality and, by God, I wouldn't be anywhere near that figure, I'd be way past it. I got through to them just how often it was.

Now the floodgates had opened. The relief to see it all being put down on paper was phenomenal. I was able to tell them everything in detail because we had lived in so many different houses, that made it way easier for me. It escalated in each location, I could pinpoint it through that. If we had lived in the same house all my life, it would have been harder to remember chronologically but he had slipped up. Maybe we moved so much so that people never found out what he was, but he had actually helped me in a way he could never have known – each house had different memories and the dates we stayed in each house were easy to prove. I knew the schools, the neighbours, the news while we lived there – I had such distinct memory points.

When I told them about the computer, I remembered it as if it had happened that morning. Back then, MySpace and Bebo were all the rage. I wasn't that interested but my friend was. I gave her Dad's old computer and she only told me the year before, when we were driving to Galway, just what she had found on it.

'I've never said this to you, Shaneda, but when I finally managed to connect that computer to the internet that you gave me, you won't believe what I found.' I bet I could. A chill ran through me – why wouldn't Harry have had what I suspected she was going to tell me all about? 'There were hundreds and hundreds of images of child abuse that came through.' She'd decided not to tell me at the time, or when she offered it back to me a couple of months before. The computer was now gone but the police wanted to track it down.

'Do you know what?' I told the guards. 'I remember once that my sister Louise was sitting at the computer at the top of the house and all of those images started coming through. There were so many pop-ups in the early days of computers, do you remember that? Any time you finally connected with dial-up, your screen would be flooded with them. Louise called on Mom when she saw a film there of a baby being raped and Mom just told her that's what it was – it was a pop-up. Louise was traumatised and she was just brushed aside.'

The guards never did find that computer.

When I made my statements, they didn't know where Harry was and that was obviously a problem as they needed to talk to him. This affected my sleep so I went back to the GP to try and get some help. I told him that I had been making my statements and he told me that I needed to up my medication.

No sooner had I left the doctor than I got a phone call. It was from a woman who used to be friends with Rose, but they'd fallen out some time ago.

'Shaneda,' she said, 'I know where your father is. I saw him in a Limerick pharmacy where I went to collect some medication for my mother. I think I know where he lives.'

She told me what she knew and I passed it onto the police – she was right. It had been Harry and now that we knew where he was, the police could make their move. Suzanne told me that the Detective Sergeant didn't want to meet me until he had interviewed Harry – he didn't want an image of me in his mind. I had this thing in my mind that they would go and arrest him – when I was told that they had 'invited' him in, I went ballistic. I rang the detective who didn't want to meet me yet – DS Kevin O'Hagan – and let loose.

'Invited? Invited?' I was enraged. 'Inviting him like he's someone special?'

'No, Shaneda,' he told me, 'I find it better than arresting them to invite them in and make them feel it's not something as big as it is.'

They wanted to get him before he knew.

When Rose found out, she was back on the phone, whining again. 'Shan, I thought you said you weren't pressing charges?'

'Well, Rose, it's a woman's prerogative to change her mind.'

She was still in complete denial.

I told the guards, 'My dad will come here and he'll admit everything.'

'That's not really very likely – not when he sees how many charges there are.'

'I'm telling you, he'll admit it all.'

'What makes you think that?'

'Because he's the most arrogant, ignorant, cocky person you will ever meet in your life.'

My friend Lorraine and others were all interviewed, the ones who were in the story, Rose, my sisters – anyone who I had named. Although she didn't know what I had told the guards, Lorraine said the same thing about Harry: 'Her dad will come down here and tell you it all.'

'What makes you think that?' they asked her too.

'He's Harry.'

Rose was going between whining about how awful her

life was and roaring that she was seeing everything being taken out of her control.

'What is the matter with you?' I asked her. 'Why are you this way, Rose?'

'I'm SICK of this! When is it going to end?'

'Very soon, Rose, very soon.'

I knew Harry was going to be getting interviewed in a week but I'd be damned if I would tell her the date. Let her stew for a little while longer.

And I'd been right.

'Shaneda, I can't believe it! Your dad came in and admitted everything – even with his solicitor there. You were right, I've never seen it before,' said DS Kevin O'Hagan.

'He's trying to trick all of you – he'll say how sorry he is, how he'll get more therapy.'

'He did cry.'

'Am I meant to feel sorry for him? He's only crying because he got caught, Kevin. He always told us, if you commit the crime, you have to do the time. He also used to say, admit the crime, you'll do *less* time. He's not sorry, he's just annoyed.'

'How did you know he would admit it all?'

'I know him best out of anyone in the world. He became my world. He made me adore and love him so I know exactly what he's like.'

'How did he keep you under such control?'

'I don't know. He never threatened me, he just told me that he'd go to prison if anyone found out.'

'Shaneda, that *is* a threat to a little child.'

I'd never looked at it that way but it was a very clever threat. The family would be broken apart by me, not him, if he was sent to prison.

CHAPTER 19

Impact

———

I had every faith in the judicial process and I genuinely believed from the start that it would go to court. Before social media, especially Facebook, none of us in Ireland really knew what we were entitled to, what rights we had, but now, all of a sudden, you could get information. You could see what wasn't right and you could see what you should be getting, and that made me think that I was doing the right thing and the right thing would be done by me.

DS Kevin O'Hagan gave me a copy of my statement one day – I came out of the cop shop, crossed the road and put it in the bin. I knew what had happened, I didn't need dozens of pages to tell me – I'd had enough of my own story. I felt strong. I'd been so eaten up with the guilt of keeping secrets, of the way Irish society thought that shutting up about abusers was the right thing to do, and now that was over.

I didn't cry once. I was doing it for something else. At that moment, I knew he would never stop, I knew he would always do it for as long as he got away with it. When all of this came out, he was working in a school kitchen – they always find a way, who knows what he had planned?

I want to emphasise that when you are groomed and abused, you firmly believe you are the only one. They make you their world so you believe you are important, they love you, you are special to them and you are the only one in that position. I had an amazing experience with the guards, every single one of them, and they all came through for me. I know people will find that unusual, but it is genuinely what happened to me. They were incredible and the day I found out the prosecution was going ahead, I knew that they were as happy as me.

Kevin O'Hagan called me down to the station: 'Shaneda, the DPP [Director of Public Prosecutions] came back and it's a prosecution.'

I'd assumed I would be getting one anyway.

'Two hundred and twenty-seven charges.'

'Sample charges?

'No, those *are* the sample charges. There are over 2,000 charges.'

'WHAT?'

My stomach was churning. This was unheard of.

They went back to Harry and he wanted to deny eighteen of the charges. *Eighteen.* It was all to make it seem like I was older when he had done it, to make it look legal and consensual. I was dumbfounded. Why not deny all 227? The DPP came back and said that my memory was so crystal clear, they were charging him with all of the counts.

It was the following April in 2011 when he was charged. My sister Eve spotted the car outside the cop shop and saw him going in. It took twelve hours to charge him, there were that many counts. He volunteered to go into prison on remand just as I knew he would. Bail had been set at £10,000.

I phoned Rose and said to her, 'If you DARE to put up bail for him, I'll come out and burn your house to the ground, do you hear me?' I'm doing myself no favours saying that, I suppose, but it's the truth. She was still pretending she was on my side, but I'd never known it in the past and had no reason to believe it now. My sisters had told me before Harry was on remand that she was going for counselling hours away and it was an eighty-minute drive to even get there.

'That's an awful long way to go, don't you think?' I said to them. 'Do you think maybe she's not telling the truth by any chance? She's with him.' I went onto Google Maps and typed in her address and the address I knew Harry was staying at. What a surprise: eighty minutes. There was nothing about the pair of them that could shock me. Now others were seeing what I meant.

Kevin O'Hagan said to me, 'Shaneda, I got to see what you mean about his arrogance. When I was bringing him through the prison gates in handcuffs, where he had worked for twenty-six years, he looked at the fella at the gate and said, "I bet you never thought you'd see me on this side." You were right.'

Harry knew the system and he played it. He knew he would get done for this, so why not start his term straight away then it would be taken off his sentence? He appeared twice in Ennis Court House in April. My friend Aoife and I went into the corner shop to buy a local paper. I grabbed it off the shelf and took it back to the car, where we went straight to the court pages, but there was no mention of it.

We closed the paper and only saw the front page for the first time. In screaming letters, it said:

CLARE RESIDENT CHARGED 227 TIMES

It was then that I knew it was bigger than I had imagined. He pre-signed all of the pleas and it all flew through – I believe he thought the quicker it went through, the less notice would be taken. He was on remand until the trial, but Rose was still not giving up on him. The night he was taken in, she had been to Shannon to collect his car –

making sure her priorities were right, I guess. She rang to let me know.

'I'm going to sell it,' she told me for some unknown reason.

'What are you telling me for? Are you giving me half the money or something?'

'I am so SICK of all this bullshit!' she exploded.

'Really, Rose?' I said, calmly. I hung up the phone and never spoke to her again until a few years ago. It stung that she could minimise what he had done to me by saying it was all 'bullshit'.

I thought the courts were like schools and that they closed down for summer from July – when I was told by DS Kevin O'Hagan that the date of the hearing had been set for 29 July 2011, I was shocked. I wouldn't have the summer to come to terms with it, it would be here before I knew it.

'July?' I repeated to him. 'Maybe I should have known.'

Aoife and I had been to a fortune teller in the January. I don't really believe in all of that, but this lad was famous all over Ireland and you had to wait months to see him. Aoife was in there for two hours, but with me, it looked like he didn't even try.

'I can't read you,' he said. 'All I can say is that you have chosen your own destiny and you'll get the justice you're looking for. I can read you after that, after July.' I'd told Aoife it was a lot of shite, but now I was wondering.

I had my friends around me, I had all their support, and the police were fantastic. A week before it kicked off, Kevin O'Hagan drove me to Dublin so that I could see the court. I wouldn't have to testify as Harry had admitted pretty much everything, but I wanted to be there when it took place. Kevin brought me in. I had never been in such a place. It was a huge, circular building with four storeys and balconies overlooking the forecourt. I don't remember going through security, I don't remember much of it other than thinking, *this is where Harry Daly will face up to what he's done.*

The next step was for me to write a Victim Impact Statement (VIS). This was by far the hardest thing I had ever written. I didn't fully understand what it was – there was no one to turn to, I couldn't find out about a VIS, no one outside the justice system really knew about them in Ireland. Kevin said it had to explain the impact on me; it could be one page, fifty pages – try not for fifty or people would fall asleep though, he said – but it really had to show what I had been left with. I wasn't allowed to mention anyone else, just me. I agreed that I would read it out in court. If I had known then what I know now, I would have written about the actual impact – it would have been different, I would have used different words as I didn't actually know then what the impact had been.

VICTIM IMPACT STATEMENT

I was sexually, emotionally and physically abused by my father from a very young age until three months before I turned 18. From the age of 12 it became daily if not two or three times a day. I never had a childhood and can never get it back. Everyone got to play with their toys while my father was playing his own sick game with me. He tried again to sexually assault me when I was a 26-year-old grown woman with three children. He has never been sorry – just sorry I told.

My mother has known all this but yet she still stayed with him up till I went to the guards last year. I have had no contact with my mother or sisters in months. I was treated like a housekeeper and practically raised my sister, who was born when I was 15. Her cot was put into my room when she was a few weeks old. My father was violent, hitting me with bamboo sticks, belts and fists. My two sisters were never hit or treated badly. He liked control and would get me to remove his shoes and socks when he came home from work. I didn't bother telling anyone because he had a respectable job as a prison officer and I thought no one would listen to me. I never called my parents mom and dad and now know they didn't deserve the titles.

I have never had counselling until recently as I've been terrified to release all the emotions from inside me. I'm afraid if I start to cry, I will never stop. I have been told I have mental health issues and have to start seeing a psychiatrist in August to start dealing with all this and the idea of dealing with it frightens me. I've never felt loved by my parents and that has obviously impacted on my relationships with people. A simple argument could devastate me, making me feel rejected by everyone. I've been over obsessive with my five children, wanting to know their every move for fear they would be hurt. My life has been one nightmare. I don't sleep properly, I need sleeping tablets and I take antidepressants.

There is not one day ever, even on happy occasions, that I do not think of what he has done to me. I get a shiver up my back and anyone who knows me well knows what it means. I feel ugly, I don't like people getting too close to me. I have stayed at home for days at a time because I don't want anyone to see me. I have even started to cry around my relations as I feel so ugly that I will make them ill looking at me. The abuse has cost me my ten-year relationship with the father of my first three children and has affected my current seven-year relationship because of the stress of the past few years, especially the last few months – if not for the support of my partner and friends around me daily, it would have been much worse.

I have been excluded from family occasions because my father was welcomed instead of me. I didn't get to celebrate Christmas with my mother and sisters because my father was there and I was excluded. I've always found Christmas so depressing as everyone else had family meals and I had none. I've always been made to feel I tried to destroy my family. I feel angry but have to keep it inside because of my children. I love them so much and I want them to have a happy and normal childhood unlike the childhood I had. I'm depressed, paranoid, I avoid sex, which is an important part of a relationship, but I can't stop having images of him doing disgusting things to me that no one should do to a child. Since making my statement I have been getting flashbacks of things he has done and know there is a lot more I don't remember and it terrifies me how I will cope with those emotions and memories. To everyone on the outside, I'm happy and together, but inside I feel like I'm dying. I just want to know that he can never hurt or destroy anyone else like he has done to me. People say I'm a survivor and brave, but the truth is I have to try to be brave every day to try to survive.

I should have said:

I've never grown up.

I never feel like an adult.

I always feel inferior.

I worry constantly about being judged as a mother.

The dissociation ruins my life – I'm becoming way more aware of it.

I never know where the distress will hit or what it will be like.

People call me the Ice Queen, but it isn't true.

I understand the emotions I'm meant to feel, but I can't genuinely feel them, the dissociation won't let me.

I'm known as the strong one. I will get anyone through anything, but I sometimes worry that I won't get me through.

I can't look at people's faces when I tell them what happened because it makes me realise how bad it was.

I close my eyes, I put my head down.

Only doing this book has made me see how bad it is.

My children, my pregnancies, my relationships – it touched everything.

I underestimated what you had done to me, Harry, I underestimated it all.

CHAPTER 20

Justice

———

The trial was set for 29 July 2011. The courts didn't stop for their summer recess until the end of the 30th. DS Kevin O'Hagan had told me a month before that it would be happening. The day he drove me up, I decided that I was going to stay in Dublin with my Aunt Imelda. I'd get three days on my own to clear my head away from the kids before the trial. I was going between Imelda's and Karen's (my cousin, Imelda's daughter, who I would say is my soul sister even though she's fifteen years younger than me). We were really just waiting, not talking about the court case, just drinking tea and chatting. I was on sleeping tablets, which was grand as I wasn't lying awake all night, thinking about what was coming.

Aoife and Lorraine told me that they were coming to the court no matter what I said. They knew me well. I was so against putting anyone out, even though I would be the first person to support other people. Aoife just presented it as a fact. Imelda and Karen would be there too, with Jack, my partner.

I got up at 5am on the day. It was still pitch-black outside and I let Karen's dog out. My mind wandered – maybe it had to – and I remember looking at that dog, a massive Newfoundland, and seeing the rain wash off her coat, just falling without soaking in. Every raindrop was distinct, every single one being repelled. I focus on little things, I know that, and I scan. I always know where things are in a room seconds after going in. If a friend wants to know something that happened fifteen years ago, I'll know. I might go all round the houses, but I'll know. It was a surreal moment standing there. I was thinking, *how does Karen wash her if water gets repelled?* Jack came down and we had tea. I put on black trousers, black boots, a black top and a purple woollen coat – it was the colour of suffragettes, the colour of bravery.

Imelda appeared with a golfing umbrella, two hours before I was to leave.

'Where are you going?'

'The court – and if your mother is there, I'll jump on her. I'll be there first, just in case.'

Imelda was ready for action! She was small but mighty, as I always said.

Jack drove me and Karen in, through security, then into

an area to keep us away from everyone else – a place for the victims. We got a coffee then went to an outdoor area – honestly, it was banter between me and Karen. When we got back, the garda Suzanne and Lindsey were there too. I was getting encouraging phone calls all the time.

'See, everyone's on your side, Shaneda,' said Kevin.

Not everyone, I thought. *Rose won't be.*

We were in good form. Aoife arrived, then all of a sudden we were told it was time to go into the courtroom – and to choose who would go with me. I was looking at my two best friends, my best cousin, and I chose Imelda.

I hadn't seen Harry since that day in the shopping centre and I didn't want to now, but the sense that he was in there was strong.

I went in.

Kevin was on one side, Imelda on the other just beside Jack, who I was clinging onto. I went in and I was terrified to see Harry, terrified for anyone to see me, the judge included. I kept pulling my hair over my face, making a curtain of it, trying to disappear. I sat near the back, but Kevin told me to move up another bench. My legs went to jelly, they were rattling as if I was freezing cold. I remember the judge looking at the charge sheet and he said, 'What is this?'

He was told there were so many sample charges they'd had to make more. 'I have never seen the likes of this,' he intoned, aloof and proper. He looked at me, looked at

Harry, back to me as I continued to hide behind my hair.

Imelda said, 'Look at him, look at Harry.'

'I can't. I can't do it.'

'He's standing there, Shaneda, standing arrogant as if he hasn't anything to be ashamed of.'

I still couldn't do it.

They started to read all of the evidence. When I heard things like, *I placed my penis in Shaneda's mouth*, the shame made me want to vomit. Obviously, he'd had to say it all, admit to it all, but I couldn't get over it. I was horrified to hear it out loud. They read the charges, then pieces of his statement. Kevin got up on the stand to read them, pieces of what he said, then the judge said he could not believe there was not one day when I was not abused at least once a day. He kept looking between Harry and me, back and forth, back and forth, with me constantly putting my hair in front of my face – I couldn't stop. There was then a very brief character statement, then the female barrister for the Office of the Director of Public Prosecutions (DPP) looked at me and said I would read out my VIS. I shook my head – no, I couldn't do it. The DPP barrister then read it out. I was sitting there, knowing he was there, knowing Imelda was there … when I made that choice outside about who would go in with me, that was what was in my head. They'd hear it, they'd hear it all. I told my aunt a few little things but no one else knew anything. I trusted her to be able to listen to it. I thought no one else could. Little did I know she was devastated. She was holding my hand, placing her hand on my rattling legs, totally 100 per cent beside me, this tiny little woman.

'I should have strangled your mother when she was younger,' she whispered to me.

I was shaking, covering my face with my hair, with no idea how long this would go on for. The judge said he had to think about it overnight but the hearing would have to end the next day as that would be the start of summer recess. I was very subdued after that. I'd never been in a courtroom, it was like something out of *Rumpole of the Bailey* that Rose used to watch. They seemed like another breed, something not human in their wigs and gowns, and now I had to wait on them even longer.

I knew that the next day was the last day of the courts but it was a lifetime to wait. That evening was the quietest I had ever been in my life. I felt traumatised by what Harry had said, even though it was about me. It was the fact that he had said it out loud and in those disgusting terms. I went to bed early, got up early the next day. Aoife and Lorraine had to go home as they'd only expected the hearing to be one day, we all expected that.

The second day was different, everyone was a lot more serious and they were all allowed in for sentencing. Straight away I panicked and pushed Jack in front of me. I was rattling even though I knew it was going to happen.

Imelda had told me that he did look over at me the day before. I can recall snippets from the judge – *worst case of betrayal towards your child, disgust, horrific, maximum of fifteen years.* Assault, rape, all of that blended into one. It was just as they said – no one had ever seen anything like it. I was panicking about my dad, not the judge though.

When I left, I asked the female barrister – 'I don't know what he got – what did he get?'

'Fifteen years, Shaneda – five suspended, so he's going to jail for ten years.'

'Fuck my mother,' was my first response.

It was primal; it was about her, not him. In years to come it would be her betrayal which hit even harder. I don't want to make excuses for my father, I don't want to say it was illness or sickness because it's so much more than that – he is a paedophile and that is never going to change. I firmly believe it has been in him forever and nothing will stop it. But my mother, the fact that she could choose which children to love?

There was a court reporter who told me it would be in all the papers as it was such a big story. My instant thought was, *I need to see Nanny Rooney.* My grandmother would be faced with all of this and I had to let her know I was OK. If it was going to be in every paper the next day, I wanted to let her see me, see that I was still the Shanny she loved. She used to buy the *Independent* every day and read it from front to back, politics, sports, star signs, the lot; she wouldn't miss this. I wanted her to physically see me, see that I was fine.

We were driving back from Dublin to County Clare, where she was in a nursing home. I went into her room and chatted, then brought the chair over to her.

'Nanny, I need to tell you something.'

'What's going on? Is everyone OK?'

'Yeah, yeah, they are, but there's actually been a court case. My dad's gone to prison.'

'Oh my God – what's happened?'

'He sexually abused me. I wanted you to see me, to know that I'm OK. It'll be in the paper and I had to see you before that.'

She knew nothing, no one had told her anything, and she became very upset: 'Why are men so evil?' She loved her sons-in-law like they were her own, but this was too much, she was devastated. She was holding my hand, tears streaming down her face. I felt so guilty that this old woman was that way because of what I had told her. She told me a lot of secrets in that hour we were together, things I'll take to the grave with me.

'Do the women know?' She meant the older sisters by that. 'Have you told them?'

'Nanny,' I said, 'they've known for a long time. They've known since I pressed charges.'

'The pack of bitches!' she shouted. She was always like

Catherine Tate's sweary gran when she kicked off. 'The pack of bloody bitches!'

It was so emotional – Nanny Rooney was in her nineties by that time and she was weeping fit to burst. It wasn't right that she had to deal with that at the end of her life. I was holding her hand and talking with her for an hour. It meant the world to me that she was on my side and she was calm by the time I left, drinking her tea and saying she loved me.

'I'll be back to see you soon.'

Three days later, I was barred from the nursing home.

We were just leaving Dublin when my friend messaged to say there was a story online and within minutes, the whole story had hit. They had all repeated the story about the window, about him raping me from behind while I leaned out, talking to my friends.

I threw my phone away. 'I can't go back to Shannon, I can't have everyone knowing that about me,' I said to Jack.

That really got to me out of everything.

The next morning, it was in all the papers – I went up to Mace to get them. A girl coming out that I knew didn't acknowledge me and I wondered if that was how it would be from now on.

That night, Jack and I flew out to London to be with Alan. On the Monday, I got a phone call from my Aunt Marcie when I was half asleep – she was roaring at me for going near the nursing home. I didn't know what to say.

'She barred us all!' Marcie screamed.

It had taken them ages to get in and they'd had to send for Rose. I let her abuse me a bit on the phone.

'You're not to go near that nursing home unless you get my permission, do you understand?'

I came off the phone but after ten minutes rang her back: 'It's Shaneda – I just wanted to say that I would never hurt anyone intentionally, that isn't the person I am. Just because you're my aunt, it doesn't mean that you know me. I never went near Nanny to upset her, she was so nice to me and supportive, we cried together, it was a lovely moment. I don't appreciate you ringing me making out that I went there to cause war.' I got a half apology, saying she was just upset about being barred.

I spent a few days with Alan, who was upset as he maintained he should have known, he should have saved me. I told him it wasn't his fault, that abusers work on how to get away with it and he would never have known. He was younger and it was actually my job to look after him. My mind was spinning though – coming to terms with the conviction, the prison officer in prison. This was the man who had told us child rapists were scum – I was vindicated now that he was locked up and paying for his crime. He was this big be-all-and-end-all that he thought he was. I was still on a massive high.

Three cousins out of them all reached out to me: one said it was my mother who she really couldn't believe and would never speak to her again. Another apologised for never doing anything, for never acting on anything I said. The third one said that she was so sorry and that she wished I had been closer – both in distance and emotionally.

I was there for a lovely five days in London then I flew back. I was home two days before finding out Celina was pregnant, it was all back to family stuff and I guess that distracted me. I could see people looking at me in the shopping centre and I hated that, but a woman in the supermarket serving me grabbed my hand and told me I was brave, another woman hugged me so tight and said I was amazing, the woman next door sent in a bunch of flowers – little things meant a lot. It was a small place and we were the only Daly family in Shannon, I was easy to recognise. Within ten minutes here, everyone knows your business. No one ever said anything to my children. I did feel everyone looking at me.

I was told that when Rose heard the news, she said, 'It's OK, he'll be OK, he's strong.' She was still some piece of work and she still had some hurting to do to me.

In 2012, I met the journalist Alison O'Reilly and that was one of the biggest things in my life. I had been brought into Limerick Prison for not paying my TV licence. I was shitting myself, but I just couldn't pay the fine.

Dad had always told us, don't pay fines, go into prison and they let you out after a few hours. I was going to pay it when I got the money, but I couldn't at that moment. As soon as I went through the metal doors, I panicked. My chest was going, I couldn't breathe. The fella at the desk got my name and asked if I had any family members in prison.

'My dad's in here.'

'What's his name?'

'Harry Daly.'

He dropped the pen. 'Sit down there and I'll have you out in five minutes. If anything like this ever happens again, just tell us who you are.'

I was so thankful it was one of the older officers. A journalist called Debbie McCann got hold of the story and then Alison O'Reilly called to say she was doing a documentary on abuse victims in Ireland. Would I be interested? I was and so I did it with two other women. She came to meet me and did the interview. When I look at myself when I'm talking to her – we did six hours for a fifteen-minute clip – I notice that I have no emotion in my face. It doesn't move. There is no expression, even though I thought I was still on a high – I was numb. That was the first time I spoke to her. The piece came out and I also did some articles. I was still coming across as the Ice Queen even though there was a layer people didn't know, the self-critical me. I hated the photograph side or being on TV, but talking didn't bother me.

Alison said that she wouldn't be forgetting about my

case, she would help whenever she could. When I found out that Rose was now staying in a place called Port Leash, in June 2012, I told her. Alison's partner, Niall Donald, worked for the *Sunday World* as an investigative reporter and he arranged for a photographer to be outside with him. Niall just shouted, 'Rose!' when she appeared. When the photograph was sent to me, even though I knew, it still shocked me to the core. On Father's Day weekend, there were two envelopes in her hand the size of cards – one would be from her to her darling husband, but who was the other one from? Maybe she'd signed all our names.

The article basically said Rose Daly was standing by her husband. Proving she was like that made the difference. Everyone will tell you she's a lovely woman, that's all you'll hear, but it had to be shown in the papers that she wasn't like that at all.

In October 2012, I went to see my Nanny Rooney and she started screaming as soon as I walked in the door, calling me all sorts of names.

'You're a fucking liar! Get the fuck out, you fucking little bitch! Get out, I don't want to see you! Get out of here – you lied to me! Your mother told me, they all told me,' she kept roaring.

I looked at her and said, 'Are you serious?'

The more Nanny Rooney screamed at me, the more my back went up, and my last words to her were, 'Oh, fuck off!' as I slammed the door. Rose had gone to her before that last visit and given her the usual shit about me lying. It was hard because I couldn't help thinking about the times when I was about twenty and my friend Aoife and I would go on a 120km drive to see her. We'd have our coffee in one hand, a fag in the other, like some kind of Limerick Thelma and Louise, all to see Nanny, whereas people twenty minutes down the road didn't visit her. It was heartbreaking to hear what she thought of me now but I suppose I understood; she was in her nineties and her daughter was coming to tell her that it was all a lie, so what could she do?

Social media was becoming bigger. I was in a secret group on Facebook, a group for survivors, with less than one hundred people – only two of us had managed to prosecute our abusers and that was one of the things that was opening my eyes. The Director of Public Prosecutions had said no to everyone else and it was then that the horrendous stories of files going missing, not being sent in, cases being messed up really hit me. I didn't want it to be secret any longer. I put stuff up on my page, sharing articles, talking about abuse – it was the abuser's secret, not the victim's. I put up a statement saying if anyone didn't like what I was saying, they knew where to go. From that point, I did become vocal about it.

The euphoria didn't really go until 2014, once I'd had my sixth and final baby, Shane. I split with Jack the end of

September 2011, after the court case. He had been quite supportive but I completely changed. There was a lot of pressure and I couldn't even have sex for a year after I went to the guards. It all piled up on the top of the two of us basically. Then I met Adam two months later, out with friends at a friend's dad's sixtieth birthday. I had never seen him before, but we started messaging and got together in early 2012. We were engaged that October and I decided to come off my antidepressants and try for a baby. I found out I was pregnant with Shane. It was a fresh start for me as I had a clean slate with Adam regarding sex. The pressures of the court did pass once I started a new relationship in some ways although Adam did have to find out what I had been through. He was supportive, he found it hard to understand as he was from such a happy home, but he did what he could.

I was off the antidepressants once I got pregnant but then I got pre-natal depression. Everything was sort of OK, we had a lovely summer that year, I was a grandmother and Celina's baby boy Jayson had brightened up my life but something was coming.

Nanny Rooney died on New Year's Day 2014. I was going to the laying out and I was going to that funeral. It had taken me until then to appreciate that she was an old woman who had been filled with lies. The funeral would give me peace. Imelda didn't want to go as she hated seeing the face of the person when they were lying there, but Karen went with me. We were singing Rihanna all the way there, but as we pulled in the gate of the undertakers and turned to park, I looked and saw all the aunts outside. It gave me the most horrific panic attack. I couldn't breathe. I was heaving, trying to get air into my lungs, crying, telling them to go without me, but they stayed. Eventually I did calm down but then I saw Rose when I got out of the car. She ran inside but I stuck my head up in the air and walked in with my two cousins. We walked in, the coffin was there but so too was Aunt Marcie.

'Hi Shaneda,' she said, nice as anything as if none of it had ever happened. She'd had a lot of pressure on her as she was the eldest and had been Nanny's carer and I do think of her perspective, but she had been rotten to me. I went up to the coffin and looked at Nanny. She was like a movie star – as I later told Imelda, they'd done a grand job. All the wrinkles were gone and it was like Audrey Hepburn was lying in state. As I've said, Imelda didn't want to go, given she hated seeing dead ones before the funeral, and I tried to persuade her.

'You'll regret it if you don't go.'

'I won't.'

'How can you say that? Regret comes afterwards, you can't know in advance.'

Imelda did go – Nanny's other five daughters stood at the side, and Rose was floating around too. It was only family the first couple of days, lines of chairs with brothers and sisters and grandchildren and sons and daughters. I sat there looking at Rose crying, enraged that she would be like that and not care about her own child. I stared at her, willing her to feel my hatred.

Later, when we were out front, some farmers came along.

'Are you Rose's daughter?' one of them asked me.

'Imelda, is it OK to say you're my mom?' I whispered.

'Of course I'm your mom,' she said, squeezing my hand. 'Mummy Melda. You're my eldest, if anyone asks. I now adopt you, you're my daughter.'

I started spreading the word. 'You do know Rose is married to a paedophile?' I said to anyone who would listen. Most of them just looked away – they all knew, all of them.

There came the time when the coffin was due to be closed, having been brought to the church the night before the burial. We had to go up and around the coffin to say goodbye, all the family. When I stood up, I couldn't move as Rose was on the other side of the coffin and I'd have to pass her. I just froze, Karen got my hand.

'I can't, I can't.'

'You can, you can.'

I was like a little child – at the place where you stopped, to say goodbye to the deceased, my mother was right behind. I told my grandmother that I loved her, in my head, and touched her cheek. All I wanted was to kick my leg back into Rose.

The next day, in the church, the first two rows were the siblings, all wearing fur coats, then the cousins behind them. I'm nearly six feet tall, but I wore high heels that day and sat right behind Rose. You could hear the gasp. I wouldn't say a word to her, but I wanted her to know. When we went to the grave, I was on one side with Imelda and her kids – Rose was on the other side, alone. She was the only one alone in the whole place.

It was in 2014 that everything started going wrong. I couldn't get out of bed, I would come down and look at the clock and just wish the hours away until I could go back under the duvet. I wasn't washing myself, I couldn't maintain the house, I couldn't get the kids up for school. Everything was a struggle. My brain was a fog. Jack wanted custody of the kids. The high had lasted longer than I had been warned, but I was crashing now. I couldn't physically move. I had a special tool for picking stuff up off the ground – a special toilet seat, special things to actually help me do basic things.

From about November, it was bad – and Christmas was coming, always a bad time for me, just as it is for so many survivors. I would get up in the morning, look at the clock and think, *God, eleven hours until I can get back to bed*. There was no life in me, people say I had stopped moving my hands and I usually talk with my hands all the time, which meant there was clearly something wrong. I would get really upset at the table and beg Celina, 'Please can I go back to bed? I'll do anything, I'll give you anything, just don't keep me here.' I was aware Shane needed me so I took him with me a lot.

I was in the house for a year and a half. I felt dead. No feelings. Numbness. I didn't want to be doing anything. I used to tell people what I wanted for my funeral – invitation only, no one coming in and looking at me unless I wanted them there. I was deadly serious.

'I'm not going to kill myself but I want to die.'

I started keeping my appointments in the day hospital clinic and they put me on Lyrica/Pregabalin for nerves, 600mg a day, eight tramadol a day, sleeping tablets, two antidepressants and an antipsychotic. I was like a zombie. I was swollen up to eighteen stone by it all. The medication was making it worse. *I can't be taking that, I have a two-year-old*, I thought, so I halved them, then told the doctor I was stopping everything but the antidepressants. I took control as they were just throwing medication at me and not dealing with what I really had – depression in victims is different to other depressions, I truly believe that, and I also believe that therapists need specific understanding of the brain trauma we've been through. Every six months, you get a new psychiatrist and one of them told me to smoke weed to get through it. Half of them have no idea what they're talking about, but they're the experts.

The physical symptoms were a manifestation of the mental turmoil I had been through. Fibromyalgia is very common amongst survivors and that is what I was diagnosed with. I didn't know what was wrong and I didn't care. Jack was fully justified in what he did really and the judge was right in his ruling. I needed ongoing treatment and they needed stability. We told our kids they would go to their dad during the week and me at weekends. No child that age needs the burden of information that isn't right for them at the time.

We got joint custody and I kept Shane as he had a different dad. All the other three were up and running; they were teenagers and Celina had her own family. It was horrific depression after that – I mostly kept Shane in the room with me. I found it so difficult to leave that room, he could be running around or in his cot, I just didn't want to leave. Thinking of it now can bring tears to my eyes. I can't believe I got that bad. I didn't care that no one was checking up on me – even when friends called, I could see the phone was ringing but I couldn't pick it up. It was agoraphobia, looking back. I had to take control of my mental health, I had to come to that decision. I was lying in bed, rotting; I felt like I was dead inside. I wish I'd never taken my father to court. I'd lost everything. I had no one, I had nothing. My parents had everything, including each other.

I want people to know that many, many women lose

custody of their children after a court case and no one ever talks about it. From talking to survivors over the years, I know how common it is – there's no research being done, there's no research being done on any aspect of this in Ireland, but I can tell you that one in three of the women who approach me have lost custody. It's so common and it kills me. I can tell everyone I was raped but when it comes to saying two of my children went to live with their dad, it's soul-destroying. People judge, they always wonder why kids aren't with the mother, no matter what. I know it was right, but I still think people judge.

But I was sick of it. I was sick of being judged, and I was going to get myself better and make sure my voice was heard – for me and for all the other survivors out there who didn't have a hope in hell of being heard.

CHAPTER 21

Breaking and Mending

The memories come out of nowhere. I'm still terrified of car washes. The first time I sat in one without my dad, I couldn't contain myself when the water and the foam and the washers came on. I have tried to take my memories back, to smash the cycle, but not the car wash. I can't express enough that the abuse was everywhere. Sometimes I try to break the triggers, but I hate being trapped, I can't bear people on either side of me – I say the couch is made for two, not three. I don't like anyone touching me. I hate someone patting me on the head. I didn't understand triggers until recent years but, by God, I understand them now. I try to make new memories, to bring a happy new memory into things rather than let him control everything and everywhere but it's bloody hard.

I'll take the blame for everything. With friends, I would always say things were my fault and even now, writing about the abortion, I would be more concerned about what would happen to the woman who had done it than about myself. It was never talked about in this country, you would hear things but it was never openly discussed. All I knew was that I had got rid of something I thought would be a monster. I think I did feel I might never have babies again, that if you had an abortion you would never get pregnant again, but the greatest concern was to get rid of Harry's child and deal with anything else later. The problem nowadays I think is that Ireland has suddenly been allowed to do so many things at once – we were one of the first countries to legalise same sex marriage, we repealed the abortion laws, there was an influx in such a short amount of time and it has left people stuck between new ways and old ideas. We wouldn't even have been allowed to know a TV presenter was gay – they probably wouldn't have been able to be on telly anyway, but if they were, they would have to lie. I have a friend who is a lesbian and her daughter said that she didn't want any gay friends coming to the house – that sort of view was just accepted, it was seen as perfectly legitimate.

'Tell her she's being a fecking bigot!' I said. 'How dare she say that to you, to her mother.'

I have always believed that if someone is doing no harm, leave them to it, stay out of their business, and I can't see why two people of the same sex loving each other if they are both of a legal age is a problem.

I do try to understand people, to have empathy for them, but sometimes I hate that – it's too raw. People are entitled to their feelings, their grief, there's no hierarchy and I can understand that. Someone losing their cat might be the worst thing that ever happened to them – I don't have the right to say that my life is worse, my experiences beat yours. I am fine helping other abused people, it doesn't keep me awake because it fills my heart if I can help someone get through a day that was hurting them. I love telling people that how they are feeling, it is normal; to explain grooming to them. I felt like I was the only freak in the village – I wish someone had told me that there were thousands of us.

In November 2015, the journalist Alison O'Reilly rang me but I didn't laugh with her any more.

'I wish I'd never done the court case,' I admitted.

'You don't mean that.'

'I'm serious – I lost everything, everyone, I have nothing and they still have each other.'

At 8am, she called me: 'I'm on the way from Dublin. I'm going to interview your ma – I'm going to doorstep her and you're coming with me.'

Two and a half hours later, she arrived and I got in the car. It's a one-car track down to where Rose lives, exactly a mile, and I showed her where the house was, then I was dropped back to a garage to wait. I had the biggest panic attack of my life – I knew if anyone could get my mother to say something, it would be Alison, but I still wasn't sure if she could get any truth out of her. I was roaring, crying round the side of the garage. I popped two Rivotril in my mouth to manage my anxiety and went into the garage to get a coffee. This was a country, local garage. While the women were making my coffee, I don't know what came over me but I took out my phone and showed them a picture of my mother.

'Do you know this woman?'

'Yes, we do.'

'Do you know she's married to a paedophile?'

'Yes, we do. We saw it in the paper.'

'Do you know he's moving back here when he gets out?'

'Oh no, we didn't know that. Sure, that won't be happening.'

I had been saying for ages I would put signs up to tell everyone but maybe it would be easier than that. Alison came back with the photographer.

'Shaneda …'

'What?'

'I'll never forget your mother, she is actually a complete freak.' I knew she'd met the 'right' Rose.

She told me what Mom had said. The photographer had taken pics every millisecond and it showed her slowly putting her hands to her mouth. She was trying to keep information in.

'What did she come out with?'

'That it just wasn't good enough for you that he went to prison. Just not good enough at all. You want more, you want him to break his bones and bleed. That she might love you, but it doesn't mean she has to like you. He was the first man she had ever loved and *of course* she was going to wait for him and stand by him, why wouldn't she? He's paying for what he's done, but it's not enough for Shaneda.'

'God, I've heard that one all my life.'

Alison dropped me back home and I thought, *I knew it all* – but this time, the crazy bitch had said it out loud to someone else. The tears gushed from my eyes. I always knew she would never change her mind. My tears were relief. Up until then, no one had ever really believed me, but she had shown what she was to someone else.

I would never cry over her again. You lose so much when you're abused but if you can find your way back to yourself, there's a path that will give you riches. That was the moment I started moving forward with my life. I had become indifferent to him and that was an amazing feeling to have, but for my mother, I harboured resentment. Now it was gone and she was getting indifference from me too.

Alison's story about Rose was printed in the Irish *Daily Mail* on 22 November 2015 and in the January 2016, she was pushing me to have a conference for victims of abuse, and that is how Survivors Side by Side came about.

I arranged it for the day of Rose's sixtieth birthday and the next week, the Facebook page took off.

Harry had done all he could to break me, never realising that it all made me stronger than he could ever imagine. I didn't gloat, but in 2012, the summer after he was imprisoned, the best summer I could remember, I did think, *to hell with you, you loved the sun and now you're stuck in there, paying the price and I'm lying on the grass, happy.*

I realised after about five years of him being in prison that I wanted to tell him what I thought of him. I never wanted to ask, *why me?* but I wanted to tell him something. I actually even wanted to visit him then but I didn't know where he was – I'd been told he was in the Midlands by the Victims' Liaison Officer, but that wasn't true, he was in Arbor Hill Prison in Dublin and I only found out by ringing round all the prisons, asking if he was there. He wasn't allowed to contact me but I rang DS Kevin O'Hagan and told him that I wanted to write to him. He said, 'If you do, write at the end, *as per the judge's sentencing, do not contact me.*' The Victims Liaison Officer said I would have to be on his visiting card if I wanted to see him.

'Oh, I don't think so – I was the one who put him in prison!'

Somebody rang me back and they asked if it was to do with Restorative Justice – I thought that was something they only had in America, the notion of getting offenders and victims to meet to try and get some sort of reconciliation.

I was talking to her for a while and said I would get back to her once I'd had time to think about it but it seemed to me something that was to make him feel better about what he had done. It took me a year to decide because of the depression – I felt too bad to leave the house, never mind go to see him. The clock was ticking though: I knew he would be out in November 2018 as the sentence was down to seven and a half years. I rang back the Restorative Justice team and we arranged to meet in Dublin. Pauline was a lovely woman and she asked what I wanted to get out of the meeting to help me move on with my life.

'I don't have questions, I just have statements.'

'Like what?'

'I want photographs of me as a child with my brother. I've offered to pay for copies but the bitch won't give them to me. Wait, why are you writing this down?'

'Your father needs to know in advance.'

'WHAT? What gives him the right to know anything?'

'Well, if you go in there looking for answers and he hasn't thought about it all, your reaction to not getting the answer at that moment will be different.'

I did understand it even if my first reaction was to think he was calling the shots again.

'I want to know if he sexually abused anyone else. I want to know if my grandparents told Rose she had to stay with him if she got pregnant.'

Then I wondered if I knew all of that, would it fuck

me up even more? As the process went on – about four or five meetings – I changed what I wanted to say and narrowed it down to the things I needed to vomit out. To tell him how he had affected my life. He had been doing what the Building Better Lives Programme, which is therapy for men who acknowledge they have committed a sexual offence and who claim they want to change. It was developed by psychologists within the Irish Prison Service. Harry sat there and told me what he had learned through that when I asked him – in all honesty, that was for my own amusement, what had the paedophile programme taught him indeed? I wanted him to sit there and bullshit to me. It would have taught him nothing.

The last thing I wanted was for him to stay away from me and my family. Forever.

I had to make the decision as he was getting out soon, but one week I would say I couldn't go, the next week I could. I finally did it, knowing I could change my mind right up to the end, with my cousin Karen and Imelda by my side. I'd dreamed of asking for hot tea and throwing it in his face, but that was just a fantasy that would never happen. I'd heard someone recommend that the survivor be in the room before the perpetrator was brought in and to stay there when he went out – when I thought of my legs in court, that seemed like a brilliant idea.

It was a long table with us meant to be apart from each other but across.

Far too close.

'No, he can get up to that end,' I told them.

I had my back to the door when, next thing, I could hear him come in. Then there was sniffling and I knew he was crying. I felt him passing. I had my head up, my hands planted on my eyes, keeping my poise.

I looked at him.

He looked at me. Snivelling. His eyes were the same, but his face had skin hanging from it with age – it was telling on him, sitting there in his tracksuit.

'How are you?' he wanted to know.

'Fine – apart from a few things, I suppose.' I paused. 'Like, you destroyed my childhood. I can never get that back. You destroyed my confidence. I feel inferior to everyone. I feel judged. I feel pain. I wanted to be a guard, you knew that. I came home from school every day and you raped me – how was I to keep going with anything when that was happening? How's that for starters, Harry?'

I was calm actually and it was the first time I had said the word 'rape' to him.

'You took sex away from me, I absolutely hate it.' I felt good saying that part to him because he had always told me that he would teach me how to enjoy it. Well, that had never happened.

He was whimpering, pathetic. He told me that he had moved me about so that I never had anyone to trust, that he had planned things well before they happened, that he had ruined my relationships whenever he could, that he tried to make me trust only him. I do think his downfall was ever moving me to Shannon, where I met my friends so that rang true.

'What did you learn on your programme, Harry?'

'That I thought it would make me happy.'

'That you thought *what* would make you happy?'

'Touching you.'

'You thought touching your own little girl would make you happy? You thought abusing your own little girl would make you happy? You thought raping your own little girl would make you happy? Did it, Harry? Did you have a good time? Did it make you happy after all?'

'No.'

I tried to have no expression on my face.

'But you kept at it? You kept trying to get that happiness for years and years and years?'

He ignored that question. The bastard.

'It's not easy Shanny, I'll need therapy for the rest of my life.'

It made me think he was reading something out in his mind that he had planned for a long time: those were words he had learned.

'That's an awful shame, isn't it? Still, I'm sure Rose will help you through it. Maybe this will cheer you up, Harry, though ... I'd like to tell you that you have inspired me to become one of the biggest advocates in

Ireland to help victims of sexual abuse. Fair play to you!'
I snapped.

His face dropped.

'It was what I was born to do – to make sure that people
like you don't hurt anyone again.'

There was then a gap that I was determined not to fill:
let him stew.

'Is there anything else you want to say?' asked Pauline.

'No, I'm done.'

I got up and walked out of the door even though I'd
planned to sit there until he left. I hadn't needed it. I poured
Rescue Remedy down my throat as soon as I got out, but I
had done it. He had that grooming power over me and that
was my moment. It felt good that I got everything out of
me in that hour. I couldn't tell you the whole conversation
but at least I know the highlights. I went back to Imelda's
and was on a buzz – I was on *Today with Claire Byrne*
that night on the radio so it was quite the day.

The first thing Claire asked was whether it had been
worth it.

'It was definitely worth it as I had been through so much
with depression. I started fighting that two years ago and
decided to get my life back,' I told her. 'I'd never had the
conversation with him that he had damaged me in any
way or that I was different. I didn't think the same as other
people, I didn't act the same as other people in certain
situations and I just wanted him to know that. I didn't

feel scared there today – it was there seven years ago, but today, it did not bother me.'

The next day I was distraught over some of the things he said until I realised that would be exactly what he wanted: he would be hoping I would be sitting there, my brain wrecked. He purposefully said those things to get to me again and I wouldn't give him that. He had never been a father to me, he was never even a man. He had tried to break me and I couldn't lie, there were times when I had thought of holding my hands up and saying, 'Well done, Harry, you did it.' But those moments were nothing compared to the strength that I knew could run through me. There would still be dark times ahead. I would need to learn how to harness that strength and make it work for me.

CHAPTER 22

Survival

In 2016, I started to do some media to raise the profile of sexual abuse in Ireland – I was in a secret group and I didn't want it to be a secret any longer. I became aware of social media in 2011, the year he was locked up, that it was the way of getting information out there that you couldn't get anywhere else. It's important for parents to offer support – if my mother had done that, my life would be totally different.

I was getting more and more people coming to me for help. When I set up Survivors Side by Side on Facebook, I expected a few people who had been abused to come forward, but there were mothers too, which I found shocking and surprising. I told them how much of a difference they could make. I was told that the Rape Crisis Network Ireland had seen Central Statistics Office figures which showed that the Director of Public Prosecutions took on fewer than 3 per cent of cases in Ireland. Lots of people were writing to me that their files had disappeared – they had gone in and made a statement but it wasn't there; files were lying on desks for years. As I was reading all the other cases, similar to mine, offenders were getting two years, seven years, ten years. There was no consistency and that annoyed me so much. It was a lottery. I decided to start a petition. Abusers were getting glowing references written for them to be read out in the courts, all these flowery words saying they were of good character, but no one ever asked what the victims were like. I emailed every single one of 141 TDs, members of the Irish Parliament.

In the midst of my depression in September 2014, I was told by friends to go and watch *The Late Late Show* with three women called the Kavanagh Sisters on it. These three women had changed the course of history regarding abuse in Ireland as they had been named and pictured despite their abuser – their father – trying to take out an injunction forbidding it. Now they spoke out everywhere. They weren't all misery and I liked that. I contacted them on Facebook and they came to see me the same month I had seen them on that show. They gave me a book on gratitude, where you say every day what you are grateful for, no matter how small, and asked if I would write a piece on my mom, which I did. At the end of it, I wrote, '*I don't think this is something I will ever get over.*'

At the end of 2014, I was in the Kavanagh sisters' house in Dublin. We'd formed a friendship over social media and when I reread that line, I realised I had moved on – I was over it. I shouted it in the air, I just wasn't devastated any longer. It had consumed my life. I think once Alison O'Reilly had interviewed Rose, something shifted.

Not everything is perfect, far from it. One problem that I need to talk about is how hard it is to be in public because I hate seeing my face. I have so few pictures of me with my own kids because I've scratched me out, or cut me out, of every single one. That face is the face he saw every time he abused me and to this day, I find it hard to look at.

Harry had it easy. He was in prison still acting like he owned the place; befriending others, offering a listening ear to rapists, abusers, even a murderer. He thought he was so superior, the top man and someone who knew the system inside out. It was him dividing everything off into little parts again, all his other identities.

In January 2016, Alison O'Reilly encouraged me to organise a conference – everything happens in the East, in Dublin – and there needed to be something in the West to highlight what was going on. On the 30th of that month, it happened. At the end, we all sat in a circle and one thing came out: we didn't want to go to counsellors, we wanted to speak to someone else who had been through it. There's a shorthand you can use with other survivors that professionals don't get, no matter how many books they read or courses they attend. I talk about how my dad gave me the nod and other victims just know, I don't have to fill in the gaps. You need something, not for therapy, but just a space where you can sit down and let it all out, without judgement and without someone seeing you as a case study they can write about in their next paper.

A woman called Miriam Duffy was there from Rape Crisis and I'll never forget her words: 'Girls, ye are amazing! This is the grass roots of how women's refuges and Women's Aid and family planning and Rape Crisis all started. It's women like ye who change the world for other women.'

My dream is to have a cottage in the woods which isn't government-run, where victims can go after their court case and they can have their nervous breakdown without being in the public eye. There would be no paper trail, no social workers. And in that dream, I see all survivors standing tall, realising their abusers are nothing, that what they did was dirt.

I started writing back to pieces in the papers and I would send them to the journalists who had written them, always getting very positive and encouraging responses. On 30 April 2018, I was on *Live with Claire Byrne* again, this time about the petition. When I arrived at the studio, I saw the Kavanagh sisters. We were told Charlie Flanagan was there too, the Minister for Justice – and we were told very clearly not to speak to him. I did my piece, trying to get over to him the severity of the sentences not being good enough, and he did his little talk. All the cameras were turned away and I was looking to the side, talking to Joyce Kavanagh, when I felt someone sit beside me: it was Charlie Flanagan.

'I heard you talking about me,' he said.

'Yes, I was.'

So confident!

'I'd like to have a meeting with you.'

'That's fine by me.'

'How will we arrange it?'

'I will ring your office in the morning.'

The date was set for May 2018. I was so posh and collected – and I'd got my meeting. I wanted him to understand that the judicial system needed to be trained regarding victims. This is not a normal crime. It affects us for the rest of our lives, it is in our heads every single day. I would not advise anyone to go to court.

He said, 'The government can't be seen to influence the judicial process, Miss Daly.'

'So, how are they meant to learn?' I pushed.

'There are seminars, learning processes, all sorts of things.'

'That's not good enough, you really think that stops a paedophile? Most of them are sociopaths. They get a quarter off for good behaviour. Sure, how can they get in trouble in there where there's no kids anyway? They get references – no one gave references for me, did they? As a witness to the State, you are not seen as a victim in that court, you're just there to help the DPP [Director of Public Prosecutions]. We need to be seen as people, not just as extras in our own story. The questions they ask are disgusting. I had the perfect case but then I came out and realised the reality of it and that's where the fight in me came from.'

I did feel he had listened to me though. He was involved in a Judicial Review Committee and my points would be made. I felt as if I had fifty different things to fight for and I'd have to narrow it down. The training mattered. The sentencing – they shouldn't have told me that Harry was going to get ten years when it was actually going to be seven and a half – I wouldn't have been as shocked. I tell everyone now that they'll get a quarter of their sentence knocked off straight away for good behaviour. If I sat down and worked out how much time Harry got per abuse, I would really kick off – it would be horrendous. He got piano lessons and I got years of torture. I couldn't afford nursery fees and he was getting luxuries. I do believe prisoners should get essential education, none of them should leave without the basics, but piano lessons?

I'm shocking for banter – I've even said, why wasn't I abused by a bloody priest? I'd at least have got compensation! I don't want money but I do want recognition for what happened to me. If there is a monetary amount on it, it acknowledges the damage and I think it makes people pay more attention – money always talks.

I sometimes think that I was even more attached to Harry because I didn't want to be Rose. During the time he was in prison, I always knew she would take him back if she had the chance. She wouldn't voluntarily give up on her love story and that disgusted me.

He got out in November 2018 and I knew she would be waiting for him. I knew the date anyway as I'd been told by a Victims Liaison Officer, but later on that day, I got a call from another one saying they had meant to get in touch.

'I did mean to tell you that your dad was released this morning. I've been so busy, it just fell by the wayside.'

'Good job I knew already then, wasn't it?' I told her. She didn't even know that her own team had told me.

Another slip up, another moment that the victim was last to know.

I was fine all during the day but fearful that night that he would come for my children. He could do what he wanted to me, but not them. That evening, I felt I was getting swallowed up in the depression. By morning, I was back to myself – if he came near us, I'd kill him, simple as that. He had told me at the Restorative Justice meeting in prison in October 2018 that he would be staying in the East of Ireland – they sat in that room listening to him say that and it was all a lie, he had planned to be in the West all the time.

A couple of weeks later, I got a call from a woman I

knew whose daughter-in-law was working in a crèche and had heard a conversation going on between the manager and a parent.

'I think I know where your dad is.'

'Where?'

'Leitrim Village.'

'That's where he went the first time when I pressed the charges and the guards found him.'

I rang Niall Donald from the *Sunday World*. I'd built up a relationship with him and his partner Alison, and I trusted them both implicitly.

'I think I know where Harry is, I think he's in Leitrim.'

Four days later, I was sitting out on the doorstep and someone messaged me who I knew online.

'Hello Shaneda, I've just seen your parents.'

'Where are you living?'

'Leitrim Village.'

'Are you serious? Her too?'

'I was walking my dog the same place as I go every day and was passing some flats. There was this man up on the balcony and I couldn't see him properly because of the sun. As I passed, he said hello. I said hello back. I saw all these tattoos on his forearms. Does he have tattoos?'

'He does – from his time in the Navy, ships and anchors and things.'

'That's right. I kept walking and as I turned back, I saw your mum – she was taking him back in.'

'That would be because he was talking to another woman. Thank you so much. Can you get me their car reg?'

That woman had grown up in the same village as Rose, which meant she knew it was her for sure. I told Niall about that too. I wanted everyone in Leitrim to know there was a paedophile in town. I'd been there years before – it was a lovely place he was living, a penthouse apartment. A nice crèche for him to look at from out of his window, a harbour at the other side where kids were playing. I started to get messages from people telling me that they saw Harry and Rose out for walks two or three times a day; she never said a word, but he would boldly say hello to everyone they passed. He had his head cocked in the air with his usual attitude of being the big I am.

Who on earth had assessed that place as suitable for him to live? He was meant to be monitored, but he was overlooking a crèche. Those parents needed to know and a lot of the moms and dads in the area wrote to me and thanked me for being so open about it.

Harry had just slotted back into normal life. I was beyond furious, but when I realised that the whole village knew what he was, I felt a bit better. Let him be stared at, let her be talked about, instead of me being judged. I have learned to let things go and not let them fester in my mind. The story was all over the *Sunday World*, they were doing a grand job.

Any town or village should know if there is a paedophile living there. It's not that you don't look after your kids if you don't know, it's another layer of protection in my mind. I just want them all to know where Harry Daly is and what Harry Daly is. You know, I've always hated my name, but maybe I have it for a reason. No one can pronounce it, they always think it's Sinead. Not now. Anyone who knows about him can find me – there's only one Shaneda Daly as far as I can see and she'll always speak out about this. Harry Daly named me and in that, he sealed the deal on any peace he might ever find. He'll be hunted down because of the name he gave his daughter and that will lead people to know what filth he is.

When I see myself as a child, I want to tell me that I'll get through. A few years ago, I spoke to a little girl whose mom had found out she had been abused by her dad. I sat across from this tiny eight-year-old and it was like talking to myself. I was telling her that she would be OK. I also told her to be aware as there would be other grown-ups who would sense something had happened to her and if anyone tried to do anything, she must go to someone she trusted. It was like talking to me – one difference though, her mom believed her and she would help her.

'Do you still love your dad?' I asked gently.

'No!' was the immediate, shocked reaction.

'I'll always love my dad, no matter what happened,' I told her. 'It'll always be there in me.'

This poor girl leaned into me and whispered, 'I do love him but I can't tell anyone.'

I knew; I knew she would feel that way, as it's something no one ever really talks about. It would be eating her up as everyone hated him. People don't understand.

It's so important to break the cycle. Few people understand how strong the grooming part is. That little girl wrote him letters and she wanted him to be what she needed him to be. She was bawling, she was distraught. She blamed herself for a while but I hung onto the fact that she knew to tell. I had also thought I was doing a good thing keeping secrets, letting people think I didn't talk to Harry because of money, believing I could protect people when it was him who had done the damage.

I remember once while he was out of the house, Rose came in one day and simpered, 'Oh, Harry was so upset today. The psychologist today told him he's a pervert and he's so upset.'

Dear God.

'He's finding it so hard to accept, Shaneda.'

He would have been making out he had a disease, like it was cancer, and now he was getting help. He was the one getting support, he was the one draining the taxpayer, whereas I was just expected to work it all out by myself. Rose was claiming that it was always going to happen, Harry had no say in it, but now it would all be fine. That's the only way it makes sense to me. The pair of them were always grand because they had each other – and I was always going to be lost in the middle of it.

People think once you get the conviction, you're sorted. It's all neatly tucked away and you have justice. Wrong. You fight every single day – but, do you know what? It's worth it.

I think something has been released in me doing this book. It has been the hardest thing, but I have learned so much. I have learned why I am the way I am, how strong I am and I will never apologise to anyone for who I am, for my actions. I feel at last I am allowed to be upset. My story is out there now – read it if you want to, these are my words and they matter. I have realised I'm smart and I have educated myself. I can work things out and I can see what's needed. I don't need other people to tell me, I can take control of my own life and that's what got me here. Even though I have always thought I've done my best in situations, I can see how far I've come. If I had known back then what I know now, I would actually think I should have been fixed before I had my children. It would have been so different. If I'd had help, if I had accepted and seen the person I am before I became a mother, that would have changed so much. I love them so much but it has taken a long time to love me and it's an ongoing process. I don't really feel bitter because I truly don't believe for one second that Harry had listened to anything people have tried to teach or had any interest in it either.

He has always believed he is superior to everyone else and I have no doubt he told people what they wanted to hear while thinking they were all mugs for falling for it. He just played the game while I've never had a single second of professional help.

As I've said earlier, so many women lose custody after a child abuse case in which they were the victim. And so many of them are sectioned by their families, which is disgusting. The number who are put into acute medical units when they first disclose the abuse as well as afterwards when they are dealing with the after-effects. Their families sign them in for opening their mouths. Victims are shut up. It's easier for psychiatrists to stick a label on them – they have post-traumatic stress disorder (PTSD), they are bipolar, traumatised ... Maybe they are, but they need help – look at what they've been through and address that rather than just saying they're mad and hoping it will go away. There's an epidemic out there. Let's look at those who have gone through it and help them, rather than hoping they'll shut up and no one will have to deal with the flood of paedophilia that is ruining lives. The victims are not mentally unstable, they're broken.

The brain protects you from trauma and there are self-protections that victims need to know about. You absolutely don't have to look at everything you have been through. A little place opens in your brain when the abuse is happening and it's locked. It's locked for a reason, it's protecting you. I know now about dissociation and how useful it can be. I don't try to remember really bad things, I don't want to access them. If I haven't let them out by now, I won't ever do so. There was a situation where Harry told me that he viciously raped me in the car. I had no memory of that until he told me, just as I have no memory of the first time he placed his penis inside me. For some reason I won't look at those memories and I don't even have to know what the reason is. Maybe it's just too painful to go there. Maybe it was one of his fantasies that I would fight back – who knows? There is a value to keeping some things locked away, you'd drive yourself mad if you let it all out.

I don't think you will ever get the answer to 'Why me? What did I do? Did I do something wrong? Why did you do it?' You'll never be satisfied by what they give you. I'd rather be me than anyone else because I got through it. Somehow, I had the strength and that's enough. I'm not a heroin addict, I'm not an alcoholic. You have two choices – one road or the other and you decide which one. I took the one to keep on fighting. I'm not stuck in the past, I'm using it to move forward. I feel indifferent to Harry now. After the interview with Rose, I felt the same about her, but I don't feel indifferent to what I have learned.

Believe children when they tell you.

Listen to victims.

Support survivors.

I want mandatory training for anyone who is involved in the process to understand that child sexual abuse is a different sort of crime.

I want access to a Convicted Sex Offenders List in Ireland.

I want to change the wording in the law regarding child pornography – it's images of child sexual abuse.

Don't talk about the colour of things and the length of skirts.

Never accept anyone diminishing things – it's not just your Dirty Uncle Joe, it's a paedophile and your whole family should be up in arms.

The Irish system needs to catch up with the rest of the world, they're an absolute disgrace. I want so much and I won't stop until I get it. When sentencing, no consideration should be given to sex offenders when it comes to their age, health or their standing in the community. If sentencing is to run concurrently, the number of charges must be considered and the sentence lengthened adequately to ensure justice is served. Incentives to reduce the length of the sentence, any remission and/or temporary release should be linked to the offenders' participation and engagement in an evidenced-based treatment programme. Treatment has to be available to offenders both in prison and following their release because this will support their reintroduction into society and reduce the risk of reoffending.

There has to be specialised training for all those who come into contact with or are required to support victims of abuse (judicial, garda and frontline workers). Expert witnesses must be called in all sexual abuse cases to ensure that the court understands victim behaviour – we need to do away with guesswork and just assuming abuse is something that can be understood without delving into it. There have to be free services for those who need support, as well as adequate funding for Rape Crisis Centres and other support groups, not only to eliminate waiting lists but also to fund the much-needed expansion of their services. Dublin Rape Crisis Centre currently has a waiting list of at least nine months for people to access their services – this costs lives.

The other problem that I want to highlight here is shame in this country. Shame because no one wants to acknowledge that sexual abuse has taken place. I'm a very open person and I share my story all the time. I do it to help others and I tell them there is no need to feel shame as they did nothing wrong. All of the shame lies with the abuser. There is no doubt that Irish society needs to change. It has to be acknowledged that millions of people are affected by abuse – God knows how many in Ireland as we haven't had any research into the figures since 2002, which is confirmed by Rape Crisis Network. It's now my passion in life to help others have their voice and to try and make a difference with things that are wanted and needed by abuse victims. This campaign is strong, its goals are real and it's time that someone made a difference. You cannot overestimate how difficult it is to live with the impacts of sexual abuse. The difficulty in gaining access to appropriate services that are both affordable and local only make matters worse.

I am the person I am despite my abuser. I'm nothing to do with them. I formed myself into the woman I am, I made my own personality. I was beaten and belittled, but no more. I love nothing more than the craic and laughing, that is nothing to do with them. I picked my own music and never followed the crowds. I see the best in things and people that no one else sees. Be the wolf, not the sheep. I am me despite them and I love that. I am slowly becoming proud of myself, and a lot of that is due to helping other people through Survivors Side by Side, but I don't think I'll ever get there completely. I can only hope writing this book will help.

And what do I want most of all? I want to be happy. I just want to be happy. Nothing fancy, just happiness. I know life has bumps but happiness when it can be there is all I want. Laugh through the tears – the sadness might not disappear but you'll confuse the bastards if you're smiling through it all!

I want Harry to know this:

There is nothing of you in me. I am proud of me. I have washed myself of your sins and I am cleansed.

Everything that I am, I have made by myself. My heart, my soul, my strength is mine – and I will roar with the power I've made.

You thought you were burning me with a pain that would never end – little did you know you were starting a fire that will never die out.

My blood, my very bones, everything is created from what I have overcome, not what you did. It's all me, Harry Daly – I made me the woman I am. You were – you are – nothing.

I'm me – and, at last, that is enough. That is more than enough.

Information, Advice and Support

M uch of the focus on child sexual abuse in Ireland has looked at the crimes of the Catholic Church. This is, of course, a horrific catalogue of crime and cover-ups, but I feel that it has often resulted in other cases being minimised or even ignored. It's hard to find figures, but as with every other country, instances are hugely under-reported and it's nigh on impossible to get a conviction.

In 1999, *The Irish Times* published an article which quoted Marie Keenan, an expert on child sexual abuse, and said: 'Men who perpetrate abuse have not dropped in from outer space. They are men who are born here, of Irish parents, reared in Ireland, they came through an Irish education system, are not all mad and don't have psychiatric disturbances.'

That is what we all have to face up to and until we do, no child is safe, no survivor is supported.

My Facebook page Survivors Side by Side is a private one but all are welcome. It is a place to be open, to vent, to get support – but it is also a place where you can just read the stories of other survivors and wait until the time is right for you. The page is for anyone at any stage of their journey. I set it up because I fully understand what others are going through and would like to help anyone who needs support. But it's not solely for victims of child abuse, it's also for the victim's family and friends, who may be looking for help to support their loved ones. Only members can see what is posted on the page, not because there is any shame in what we have been through, but because I want it to be a safe space.

Other support can be found through the Sexual Violence Centre Cork, Limerick Rape Crisis Centre, Galway Rape Crisis Centre, Sligo Rape Crisis Centre, Dublin Rape Crisis Centre and Rape Crisis Network Ireland.

I find it very hard to talk about what I've achieved, which is why I've asked my good friend Ruth Maxwell to do it for me. I don't want this to be seen as me being full of myself – I just want to show different ways in which voices can be heard.

Ruth says: 'Shaneda has spoken on radio and TV many times, both in Ireland and in the UK, and in particular on *Today with Séan O'Rourke*. Coincidentally, that's where I heard her for the first time and I knew I needed to speak with her. After she participated in Restorative Justice with her father, she was on the Claire Byrne show discussing that and her petition for longer sentences for sex offenders. She has written many articles and was mentioned in the O'Malley Report [a report which looked at the protections in place for vulnerable witnesses in the investigation and prosecution of sexual offences]. On International Women's Day 2019, she spoke at Coolmine Drug Rehab Centre with other prominent speakers. On International Women's Day 2021, the launch of *Woman*, a documentary by Yann Arthus Bertrand, was released worldwide and Shaneda was a participant in that. She has been my wingwoman and very close friend since I contacted her after hearing her on *Séan O'Rourke* in 2018, and been a speaker at the launch of my "Not Consent" exhibition and at most of them around the country. We participated in the new Parole Bill recording in Leinster House with TD [Teachta Dála] Jim O'Callaghan. The Parole Act is about to be commenced and we'll be at the launch of that in Leinster House. She participated in many of my meetings with government ministers, The Protective Services Bureau, Irish Prison Services, the Law Reform Commission, NGOs and many other experts in sexual violence and criminal law. She is an incredible, inspiring woman.'

I never thought I could do any of that. Some days, I'm still not sure that I can – if you don't know where to start, just take a step, one step. You'll never find out where it will end unless you try. There will be dark days, of course there will, but there will also be days when you think, I'm still here – and that's all that matters.

Shaneda x

Acknowledgements

There are so many people to thank – and so many things to be thankful for – here are a few:

Music got me through so much and I want to thank Dave Gahan and Depeche Mode for being by my side over the years. They might never know me but I have to acknowledge everything their music has done for me. The late Dolores O'Riordan and The Cranberries sang songs that made so much sense to me – when the stories of what Dolores had been through came out years after they became famous, I knew why and how she understood.

Alison O'Reilly, you are the person who has pushed and guided me through the world of speaking out about sexual abuse. You have encouraged me when I've needed it, you've been there when I thought I couldn't do it. We have shared many laughs and tears together, you are amazing in your own life and I'm honoured to call you my friend.

Sophia Murphy, my sista. Our stories are like mirrors and our bond is unbreakable.

Ruth Margaret Maxwell, my twinnie. You arrived in my life when you sipped on a glass of vino and have been in every part of my world since. We've become inseparable, advocating and taking on the system, and I know we'll be friends for life.

The Kavanagh Sisters – Joyce, June and Paula, you have been a lifeline to me since 2011. You took me on as a younger sister and have shown me such amazing love and support.

Wendy Eichel, you have always been so supportive and a major part of my experience with the Restorative Justice experience. I honestly don't think I could have gone through it without your invaluable help and advice.

Marie Barcoe, another warrior I have met on my journey and someone I now consider family. I've definitely adopted you as my sister from another mister!

Laura Witherow, we've never met (hopefully one day) but the bond we share means the world to me and I would be truly lost without you. Another adopted sister to me.

Lorraine, Aoife and Susan, my lifelong friends, you've all been there for me no matter what, putting up with my madness for years. I'll love you all forever.

Alan, my brother, you've been there for me throughout

it all and you still are. I know you'd do anything for me and I'll be forever grateful that you're in my life.

Imelda, you took me in as one of your own, you have always believed in me, loved me, and supported me. There are no words to thank you.

Karen, Marilyn and Aine, truly my soul sisters. We've all been through so much together and we know we'll be there for each other, no matter what.

My children, the truest loves of my life, you are the reason I made it through the hardest parts of my journey.

Miriam Duffy, you have a heart of gold, and the energy you put into running the Limerick Rape Crisis Centre is immeasurable. You make everyone feel important but you've also always got time for a cup of tea with me – and that matters a lot!

Ingrid Wallace was the first person I met at the Limerick Rape Crisis Centre when I was only seventeen. Back then, I found it so hard to look at people, which was why I could only communicate with her through letters. I had many years of knowing Ingrid and always brought women to the centre knowing that she would do her best for them. Ingrid sadly passed away in 2018 and her loss was felt keenly by everyone. I wish she could have seen me tell my story and know how much she meant to me.

Hazel Larkin, you are an amazing person, a survivor who helps educate midwives on the trauma of abuse victims and how triggering it can all be for them. We have worked closely on many projects and I consider you a new lifetime friend. Your work matters so much and I only hope you get the recognition you deserve for it.

Lavina Kerwick, I first heard you on *The Gerry Ryan Show*. You were the first person I had ever been aware of speaking about rape on Irish radio. It's thanks to you that we even have Victim Impact Statements in this country. I love and admire you for all you have done for us.

Jackie, my neighbour who has kept me sane while I've been writing this book. Our chats every morning as we've had a cup of tea on our doorsteps have helped me more than you will ever know.

I would like to give my sincere thanks and gratitude to Suzanne and Lindsey at the Shannon Garda Station. They took my statement as people, not as guards, and made it a very personal and supportive experience. Special thanks also to Detective Sergeant Kevin O'Hagan, who investigated my case, fought for me and made sure Harry Daly got the maximum sentence possible.

For everyone on the Survivors Side by Side page – you make it what it is and we make each other what we are.

Thank you so much to Beth Eynon at John Blake Publishing who has been such a support, who has believed in me and gave me this chance to tell my story and hopefully, help others. To Jane Donovan and the rest of the team who have worked so hard – I am eternally grateful.

And finally, my ghostwriter Linda Watson-Brown – I

want to thank you sincerely for this amazing journey we have taken together to tell my story. You have helped open pieces of me that I never knew existed. You have brought me from my past to my present and made me feel proud of who I am. Thank you so much x.